CANDICE OLSON
FAVORITE DESIGN
CHALLENGES

PHOTOGRAPHS BY BRANDON BARRÉ

Houghton Mifflin Harcourt
Boston • New York

Published by:
Houghton Mifflin Harcourt
Boston • New York
www.hmhbooks.com

For information about permission to reproduce selections from this book, write to Permissions, Houghton Mifflin Harcourt Publishing Company, 215 Park Avenue South, New York, New York 10003.

www.hmhbooks.com

The publisher and the author make no representations or warranties with respect to the accuracy or completeness of the contents of this work and specifically disclaim all warranties, including without limitation warranties of fitness for a particular purpose. No warranty may be created or extended by sales or promotional materials. The advice and strategies contained herein may not be suitable for every situation. This work is sold with the understanding that the publisher is not engaged in rendering legal, accounting, or other professional services. If professional assistance is required, the services of a competent professional person should be sought. Neither the publisher nor the author shall be liable for damages arising here from. The fact that an organization or Website is referred to in this work as a citation and/or a potential source of further information does not mean that the author or the publisher endorses the information the organization or Website may provide or recommendations it may make. Further, readers should be aware that Websites listed in this work may have changed or disappeared between when this work was written and when it is read.

Trademarks: All trademarks are the property of their respective owners. Houghton Mifflin Harcourt is not associated with any product or vendor mentioned in this book.

Library of Congress Control Number: 2012954769
ISBN: 978-1-118-50446-8 (pbk)
ISBN: 978-1-118-55377-0; 978-1-118-55385-5; 978-1-118-55372-5 (ebk)

Printed in the United States of America

DOR   10 9 8 7 6 5 4 3 2 1

Book production by John Wiley & Sons, Inc., Composition Services
Book design by Tai Blanche
Cover design by Susan Olinsky

Note to the Readers:
Due to differing conditions, tools and the individual skills, Houghton Mifflin Harcourt assumes no responsibility for any damages, injuries suffered, or losses incurred as a result of following the information published in this book. Before beginning any project, review the instructions carefully, and if any doubts or questions remain, consult local experts or authorities. Because codes and regulations vary greatly, you always should check with authorities to ensure that your project complies with all applicable local codes and regulations. Always read and observe all of the safety precautions provided by manufacturers of any tools, equipment, or supplies, and follow all accepted safety procedures.

To Pyper and Beckett,

For giving me my toughest, funniest, most

rewarding, and truly favorite challenge yet …

Motherhood

andice Olson is one of North America's leading designers and most recognized media personalities. As designer and host of *Divine Design with Candice Olson* and *Candice Tells All,* she is a favorite with viewers on W Network in Canada and HGTV in the U.S. Each week she brings a wealth of design experience and an attitude that is smart, witty, and truly unique into over 115 million North American households.

After earning her degree from the School of Interior Design at Ryerson University in Toronto, Candice launched an exciting commercial and residential design business. Considered "the one to watch" by *The New York Times,* Candice continued to receive accolades and media attention for her distinctive and exceptional work.

Candice's foray into television began when a local TV station profiled one of her award-winning design projects. Her unique approach to residential design and engaging personality led to a weekly stint as a design contributor to the show. Viewer demand for "more Candice!" led to the creation of the hit series *Divine Design with Candice Olson.* Candice and the show quickly won a huge and loyal audience and went on to achieve a milestone of over 200 episodes after eight seasons. *Divine Design with Candice Olson* continues to receive rave reviews and recognition around the world, including the more than 160 countries where the series has aired.

In 2005, Candice launched "The Candice Olson Collection," her own successful brand of licensed product lines, including upholstered furniture, fabrics, wallpaper, lighting, carpeting, case goods, and bedding. Candice's signature style is one she describes as "a fusion of traditional form, scale, and proportions with the clean, crisp, simple beauty of modern design." For more information, visit www.candiceolson.com.

The continued demand for "more Candice!" brought her to wider audiences through guest appearances on television shows such as *The Today Show, Live! with Regis and Kelly, The View,* and *The Oprah Winfrey Show.* Candice writes a bi-weekly newspaper column syndicated in over 400 newspapers across North America and is a frequent contributor to design magazines both in Canada and the U.S. For two seasons, Candice has been featured as a Celebrity Judge for the prime time hit reality show *HGTV Design Star.*

Candice spends her free time with her family, skiing in the winter and relaxing at the beach in summer. A native of Calgary, Alberta, she lives in Toronto with her husband and two children.

Table of Contents

Architectural Challenges

1

A Knockout Living-Dining Room   16

Some fancy footwork breaks up this long, narrow tunnel of a space into two stylish, elegant, and cozy zones.

West Coast Vibe   24

Soaring ceilings and cramped floor space call for some creative solutions in a new live-work loft.

Inspired by Nature   30

A tiny loft feels as big as all outdoors, thanks to some inventive small-space solutions.

Reno(vation) 911   38

Gutting two small rooms produced one awkward—and still-small—space. Time to call in the Space-Expanding Superhero!

2 Recipes for Compromise

3 All in the Family

4

Inspired by Themes

Special Spaces

5

WANT TO KNOW WHERE CANDICE SHOPS?

As her fans around the world know, Candice Olson sources out the most amazing products from her favorite suppliers across North America, and now you can gain access too!

Visit **www.candiceolsonbooks.com** to find detailed information about the materials and products from all of her spectacular rooms in this book.

Happy shopping!

INTRODUCTION

I n my 25 years in the interior design business, I can honestly say that I have seen it all and been faced with more than my share of challenges. The reasons for what makes a room or project challenging are vast and varied.

The most common reason is the space itself. A room might be too large or too small for either its original purpose or its intended new use. Bigger isn't always better in the world of design, and gargantuan spaces often feel more cavernous than spacious. I've been in rooms that felt as big as a football field and echoed when I talked!

On the other hand, it's tough to bring beauty and function to cramped quarters with low ceilings, especially when I feel like I'm taking up a disproportionate amount of the real estate. I'm a 6-footer with size 11 feet—how do I deal with a space I can barely stand up in?

Aside from size, the physical conditions—or afflictions—of a space might be the challenging factor. Moldy walls, rotting rafters, and remnants of critters stuck behind lathe and plaster walls (eeek!) might be just a few "features" of a newly purchased "quaint and charming historical home with character." These "dump to divine" transformations push the sporting adage "no pain, no gain" to its outer limits!

Truth be told, however, rooms are rooms, and no matter what the size, shape, or condition, any problem they have can be solved with equal parts brainpower, willpower, manpower/womanpower. The real challenge is often not the room itself but the people inhabiting it.

It's one thing to understand and identify one's own personal wants, needs, and sense of style, but having your significant other actually agree with you wholeheartedly is a rarity. Opposites may attract, but on the home front, opposing opinions can mean full-blown foot-stomping, breath-holding, the-silent-treatment-for-two-weeks war! I've played marriage counselor as often as I have interior designer, leaving me to wonder if vows shouldn't read, "For better or worse, but heaven forbid, not that ratty old black leather recliner with the cup holders"!

The changing makeup of who lives in a home also brings its challenges. Aside from their affinity for soft foods and frequent naps, a two-year-old and a ninety-two-year-old might not have many similar needs or desires, but these days they may well share a home, along with a couple of generations in between. Multipurpose/multitasking spaces serving multiple generations pose—well, you guessed it—multiple challenges. But this is where good design can really make a difference. A space that meets the needs of one and all makes sharing a home easier on everyone.

Finally, there are those "special" projects and "special" clients who leave me scratching my head, if not shaking it in disbelief and bewilderment.

My inner voice might be saying:

"I have *how long* to do this project?"

"You want me to do all that for *how much*?"

"You really want me to design your living room around your animal skull/beer bottle collection/table saw/ boxing ring/life-sized portrait of Captain Kirk," or other uniquely wonderful thing that makes a house someone's personal home?

My outer voice answers:

"No problem, I love a good challenge!"

1 ARCHITECTURAL CHALLENGES

A KNOCKOUT LIVING-DINING ROOM

CHALLENGE

The first room you see when you come into Kim and Rey's home is the long, narrow, living-dining area, which the previous owner painted bright yellow and turquoise. Rey, a former professional boxer, likes to use the unfurnished space to teach their two boys to box, but Kim, a painter and children's television director, says it's time to move the boxing lessons to the basement. They'd both like the space to be a warm, welcoming center for family life as well as a suitable place to welcome clients of Rey's boxing equipment business. But the space is more like a bowling alley than a boxing ring, and they don't know where to start.

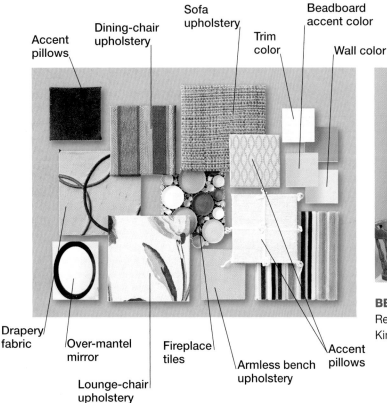

Accent pillows · Dining-chair upholstery · Sofa upholstery · Trim color · Beadboard accent color · Wall color · Drapery fabric · Over-mantel mirror · Lounge-chair upholstery · Fireplace tiles · Armless bench upholstery · Accent pillows

BEFORE: The brightly painted living-dining room in Kim and Rey's small suburban bungalow was mostly a kid zone that Kim and Rey couldn't figure out how to furnish or decorate.

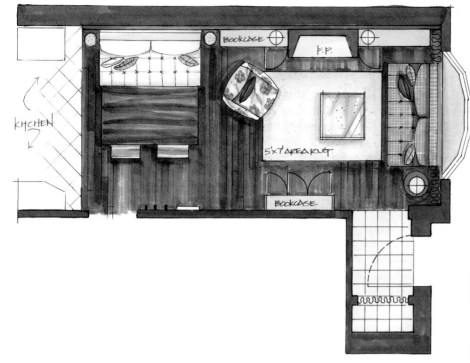

KITCHEN

BOOKCASE

F.P.

5'x7'AREA RUG

BOOKCASE

AFTER: I gave the bum's rush to those yellow and turquoise walls with knockout neutral beige and some creamy white trim. A new fireplace on one side and new floor-to-ceiling bookcases on the other break up the long, narrow space, giving the eye places to rest.

SOLUTION

- To counteract the tunnel effect, the first thing this space needs is a focal point. A gas-insert fireplace flanked by bookcases not only defines a cozy living area but also pulls your eye over to one side instead of letting it race down this long chute of a room.

- Because budget was a consideration, I used ready-to-assemble bookcases instead of custom. But to give them a custom look, I installed beadboard behind the shelves and unified the whole wall of cabinetry and the fireplace with a slab of dark-stained wood that also serves as a mantel. To add some interest and depth, I painted the beadboard a soft, watery blue.

- For some architectural interest, I also installed framed beadboard panels on the wall above the mantel and bookcases. The beadboard adds subtle texture that calls even more attention to this wall, downplaying the room's narrow dimensions.

- On the opposite wall, a floor-to-ceiling bookcase balances the fireplace and provides storage and display space. Like the bookcases flanking the fireplace, it's a ready-to-assemble unit, and I customized it with crown molding on top and beadboard paneling inside.

- To visually widen the end wall, I treated the five bay windows as a single unit. One long set of woven wood blinds, installed outside the bay, pulls down for privacy and light control. Dummy drapery panels frame the bay with tall columns of color that create the illusion of a higher ceiling.

- I anchored the dining area with an armless bench pushed up against the wall and a new, 6-foot-long pedestal table (see page 20). A pedestal table makes it easy to scoot onto the bench, and it's also easier to squeeze in a few more people around the table when you have a crowd.

LEFT: Crown molding customizes a store-bought bookcase. A floating display shelf and a unique wall-hung organizational system add function and style to the adjacent wall.

ABOVE: Nothing says focal point quite like a fireplace! I framed the gas insert with a surround of fireproof cement board painted flat black to blend with the insert's frame, then installed a beautiful mosaic of randomly sized round glass tiles. Beadboard panels set into picture-frame molding add dimension to the walls above.

BELOW: A modern chandelier with a chrome finish hangs above the dining table to provide a little visual separation between the dining room and the adjoining kitchen. The wall above the upholstered bench is the perfect spot for a gallery of family photos. Hanging it was easy, thanks to a template system—just tape the paper template on the wall, install the hangers, and hang the framed pieces in the corresponding spots!

STYLE ELEMENTS

- Kim and Rey had bought a striped ottoman in an attempt to start decorating the space, so I used it for my jumping-off point. I pulled the putty-beige color for the walls from the stripe and chose a crisp white for the trim and the ready-to-assemble bookcases.

- With all the light neutrals helping expand and enlarge the sense of space, I decided on a dark, pre-finished wood-plank floor to ground the room.

- For furniture, I chose armless and open-arm seating to help keep the look and feeling open. A tailored, tufted love seat fits right in front of the bay window, and a lounge chair with sleek, modern lines rounds out the living room seating. Petite but comfy dining chairs can be moved over to the living room if there's a crowd.

- For fabrics, I chose a beautiful floral that looks like a watercolor painting for the lounge chair and a solid, neutral tweed for the love seat. I found a stripe very similar to the ottoman fabric to use on the dining room chairs. A beautiful large-scale modern geometric for the draperies plays on—what else?—the boxing ring. The draperies are nonfunctioning dummy panels, but they bring in a splash of color at the end of the room and pick up on the blues in the lounge chair floral.

- The ring theme shows up in the fireplace surround too. The mosaic of randomly sized round glass tiles is a showstopper that brings together all the colors in the palette. I used a creamy white, nonsanded grout on the tile to avoid scratching the gorgeous glass surface.

LEFT: Round glass tiles bring modern, geometric pattern to the fireplace, and chocolate-brown lampshades and accessories pick up on the dark brown floor. The tall mantel lamps lead the eye upward, creating the illusion of higher walls, which helps the small space seem larger.

OPPOSITE: Pedestal tables are a great solution in small spaces because you can pull up chairs all around, and no one has to straddle a table leg. The armless bench also saves on space—no need to allow room for pulling out chairs.

ABOVE: This super-cool organizational system is almost like a piece of art! Pegs toggle out from the polished wood slab to hold keys, book bags, or the all-important boxing gloves.

WEST COAST VIBE

CHALLENGE

Brandon, a photographer, and Cory, a makeup artist, bought their newly built two-story loft in the heart of downtown thinking it would be the perfect place to live, work, and entertain business clients. Unfortunately, while the walls soar 16 feet high, the usable square footage is cramped and narrow, and the little bit of lighting was way up high. With inadequate storage and no organization, the loft was the very definition of pandemonium! Brandon and Cory turned to me for help in making this dramatic contemporary space an efficient and functional home and studio, with a bit of a West Coast vibe to reflect their roots.

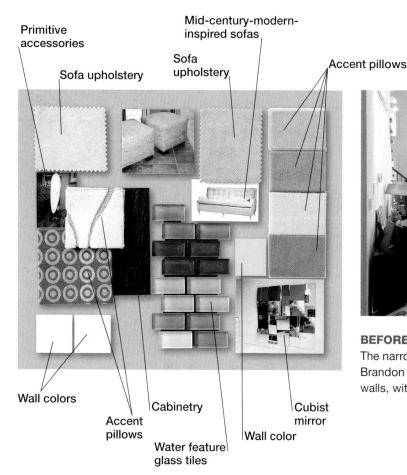

Primitive accessories

Sofa upholstery

Mid-century-modern-inspired sofas

Sofa upholstery

Accent pillows

Wall colors

Accent pillows

Cabinetry

Water feature glass tiles

Wall color

Cubist mirror

BEFORE: All the space in this new downtown loft was vertical! The narrow, open-concept main floor had no storage, so Brandon and Cory found themselves piling things along the walls, with no order or organization.

AFTER: A spectacular feature—an indoor waterfall and fireplace flanked by display shelves—tames the soaring 16-foot-wall and makes it a dramatic focal point. Dividing the floor space into zones for lounging and eating creates a sense of order in the main living area, and a cable lighting system brings light down into the room.

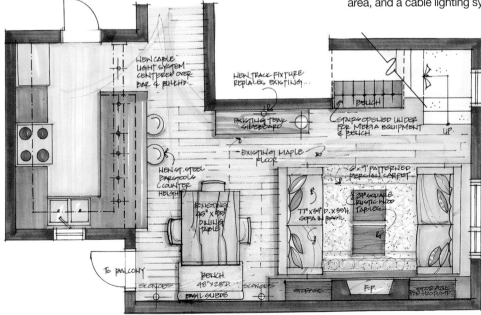

SOLUTION

- The first task is to anchor that huge vertical wall with a show-stopping focal point. I think a combination waterfall, gas-insert fireplace, and display shelves will do the trick! The water cascades down the tile face, and a water pump, concealed in the cabinetry at the bottom, continuously recirculates it.

- Mirrors—12 separate pieces—back the display shelves to reflect light and views. Nothing expands a narrow space like mirror!

- The loft desperately needed more light. I replaced the original inadequate lighting with high-tech dropped fixtures coming from a ceiling track and added a sleek, contemporary cable system over the counter in the kitchen area. The 12-volt cable has lights that can be positioned to direct illumination where it's needed. In the dining area, I installed huge, 6-foot-tall sconces. They're really intended to be ceiling fixtures, but mounting them on the wall 40 inches above the floor sends 150 watts straight up that 16-foot-high expanse. Now that's dramatic!

- To create more room for much-needed storage, I opened up the wasted space under the stairs. Custom-fitted shelves turn this area into a media center, with room for the TV, media equipment, and DVD storage.

- New furniture defines the two functional zones. In the lounging area, a pair of sofas sits perpendicular to the focal point wall, with a clear view of the television on the opposite wall. Between the living area and the kitchen, I installed an upholstered banquette and a table that seats four to serve as a cozy dining area.

OPPOSITE: The focal-point wall summarizes what the whole room is about: Natural elements of wood, water, and fire refer to Brandon and Cory's Vancouver roots and turn an overwhelmingly high 16-foot wall into a stunningly dramatic feature. Uplights at the base of the waterfall play up the tile, while under-shelf puck lights emphasize display items.

BELOW: Stealing some space from under the stairs carves out a niche for the TV and media equipment. The hefty leather ottoman offers more guest seating and can be moved where needed.

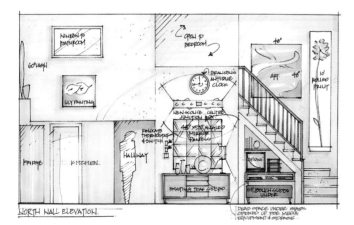

NORTH WALL ELEVATION.

STYLE ELEMENTS

- To capture that West Coast vibe that Brandon and Cory wanted, I used a vintage print of a surfer dude for inspiration. It supplied the color palette for the walls—a different color for each wall, but all in similar soft sea and sky tones.

- Boxy, 1950s-inspired sofas upholstered in two different fabrics nod to retro style. Pillows in earthy hues of sage, camel, mushroom, and putty bring in lots of texture and pattern—organic chenille, cashmere, and bold geometrics.

- For the back of the waterfall, I chose a beautiful glass tile applied in a banded pattern. A cement-board backing ensures that the feature is waterproof.

- In the dining area, I enlarged three of Brandon's photos to 48 inches square, framed them, and stacked them up the wall. The images emphasize the coastal theme, and the scale balances the impact of the waterfall-fireplace feature.

ABOVE: This Danish Modern buffet, part of the dining room set the couple already owned, combines clean, contemporary lines with the warmth of natural wood. Above it, a Cubist mirror expands space and turns reflections into modern art.

OPPOSITE: Brandon and Cory already had this sleek, Danish Modern dining table and chairs. I added the "wow" factor with dramatic sconces and super-sized prints of Brandon's photos.

INSPIRED BY NATURE

CHALLENGE

When Andy and Melinda moved from their 400-square-foot apartment to this new 700-square-foot loft, they thought they'd have plenty of space, but now they're not so sure. It's their first real home, and it also needs to accommodate Melinda's massage business. They want the space to feel comfortable and inviting and to reflect their love of the great outdoors. My challenge is to make the tiny condo feel and function like a much bigger place that's perfect for two and welcoming for a small crowd.

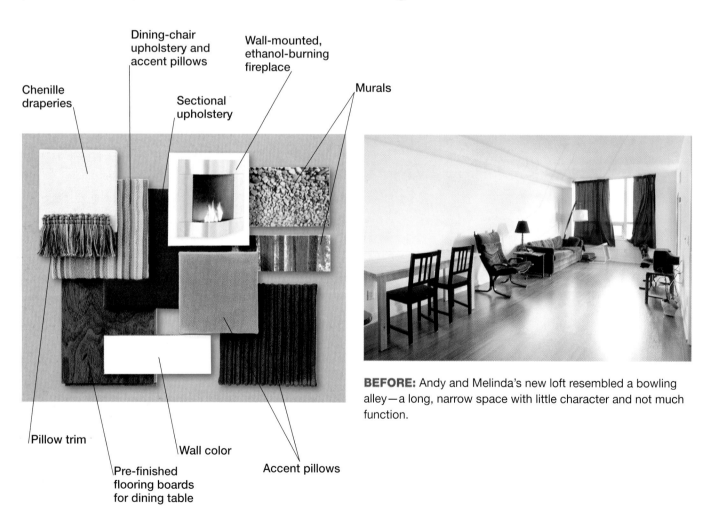

Dining-chair upholstery and accent pillows

Wall-mounted, ethanol-burning fireplace

Murals

Chenille draperies

Sectional upholstery

Pillow trim

Wall color

Pre-finished flooring boards for dining table

Accent pillows

BEFORE: Andy and Melinda's new loft resembled a bowling alley—a long, narrow space with little character and not much function.

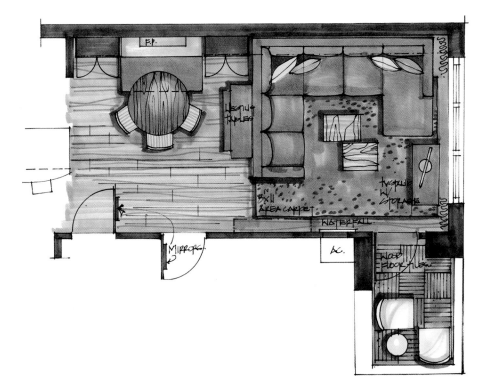

AFTER: Organizing the space into a dining area and a living area along one wall leaves a clear traffic path to the tiny deck outside. Pancake lights and shallow puck lights in the bulkhead show off the room's "wow" features—a raised fireplace and eye-catching murals.

SOLUTION

- The loft is basically one very long room, with the kitchen at one end and a wall of windows at the other. I started by dividing it into a dining area beside the kitchen and a living area that takes advantage of the windows' light and views.

- The bulkhead along one wall is the perfect place for a pair of bookcases that ground the dining area and add architectural interest. To stretch the decorating budget, I used stock bookcases and souped them up with mirror backing and glass shelves and doors.

- Between the bookcases I installed a raised fireplace to give the dining area a focal point. It burns ethanol, so there's no need for venting, which would have been impossible in the condo.

- The loft had only one junction box, so I used that to work in 16 feet of track lights along the ceiling for positionable overall illumination. Shallow pancake lights fit along the bulkhead to wash light down over the walls, and pendants accent the dining table and the living area.

- Unsightly heating and air conditioning units are a fact of condo life, but I have a fabulous solution: a free-standing waterfall feature that screens the A/C unit and adds the soothing sound of running water that Melinda's clients will love (see page 36).

- The couple needed a dining table, so I had a round table custom-built using scraps of pre-finished hardwood flooring boards.

- For seating in the living area, I chose a sectional that maximizes every square inch of space. A right-arm chaise and four additional sections make up a U-shaped seating zone that easily and comfortably accommodates a crowd. Placing the TV on a stand in front of the windows eliminates the problem of glare on the screen.

- To extend Andy and Melinda's living space outdoors, I covered the deck surface with outdoor deck tiles (see page 37). The tiles simply lock together and rest on top of the existing surface—no need for nails or glue—and they allow water to drain through when it rains.

ABOVE: A canister-style pendant fixture, one of a pair, drops light down into the room. Shallow recessed lights in the bulkhead accent the show-stopping murals that bring character and definition to the wall.

BELOW: With three upholstered chairs and a bench, Andy and Melinda can seat at least five people around their new round, pedestal dining table. A sleek little pendant fixture brings light down into the room and picks up on the stainless-steel finish of the ethanol-burning fireplace frame. When Melinda has clients over, a massage table replaces the dining table and chairs.

STYLE ELEMENTS

- To pay homage to Andy's love of nature and the great outdoors, I covered the long wall under the bulkhead with two murals, one of river rocks and one of tree trunks. Applied like wallpaper, the murals offer a high-impact, low-cost way to completely transform the space, and the large scale makes the images seem almost abstract.

- The murals provided the key to the color palette: a neutral stone color for the remaining walls, a rusty orange for the sectional, and bark-, moss-, and stone-color fabrics for pillows and dining-chair upholstery.

- For light control, I hung woven wood blinds with a weathered timber finish and backed them with blackout lining. Pinch-pleat draperies of creamy stone-color chenille fall from the ceiling to the floor, framing the windows with some softness.

- I used the wall and doors opposite the murals for display, with three narrow shelves that pick up on the color of the bookcases and two sets of decorative framed mirrors that reflect light and add the illusion of space (see page 36).

- A suede area rug and wood-block cubes emphasize the nature theme in the living area. For the TV stand, I chose a contemporary glass-and-metal unit that takes up little floor space and is see-through so it helps make the room feel larger.

RIGHT: A dramatic mural anchors the living area and inspired the loft's new color scheme. The super-comfy sectional provides lots of seating in a small space, and its clean, straight lines help keep the feel of the space open and uncluttered.

LEFT: A super-sleek, ultra-cool free-standing waterfall hides the unsightly air-conditioning unit beside the door to the balcony. Floating shelves turn the adjacent wall into a gallery. Dark-framed mirrors on the doors help break up the expanse of neutral color with light-enhancing reflections.

BELOW: Deck tiles laid over the original balcony surface give a warmer, more finished look to this tiny outdoor space. A petite metal table and chairs offer the perfect spot for morning coffee or late-afternoon drinks.

RENO(VATION) 911

CHALLENGE

You'd think that gutting two small rooms would open up one nicely sized space, right? Well, not in Hanem and Cameron's little semi-detached house. It's their first home, and they threw themselves into renovating it. But after tearing out the walls on the first floor, they were dismayed to find that not only was the space still cramped, it was also somewhat dangerous, with an open staircase smack in the middle of it. Time to call in the Space-Expanding Superhero to rescue this renovation!

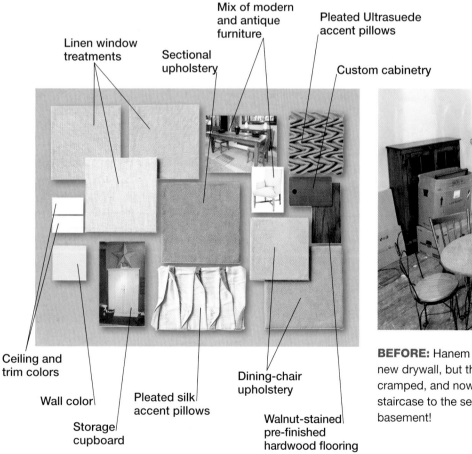

Mix of modern and antique furniture

Pleated Ultrasuede accent pillows

Linen window treatments

Sectional upholstery

Custom cabinetry

Ceiling and trim colors

Wall color

Pleated silk accent pillows

Storage cupboard

Dining-chair upholstery

Walnut-stained pre-finished hardwood flooring

BEFORE: Hanem and Cameron had torn out walls and put up new drywall, but then they were stuck: The space still seemed cramped, and now it was awkward to boot, with the open staircase to the second floor and a gaping hole leading to the basement!

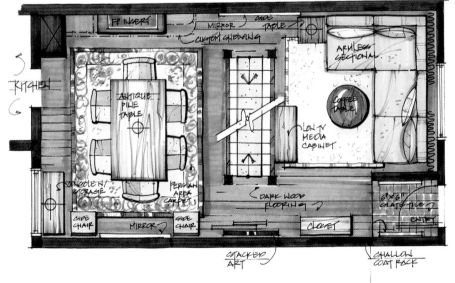

AFTER: New paint and trim and continuous dark-wood flooring unify the entire space, and new custom cabinetry puts storage and a focal-point fireplace where nothing existed before. I framed the stairs with railings, using simple square balusters to preserve the feeling of openness between the dining area and the living area.

ABOVE: A long, low, armless sectional takes up a minimum of visual space, but provides lots of comfortable seating. An antique pine blanket box, one of the many pine pieces that Cameron collects, serves as a coffee table. Banded linen draperies and simple sheers soften the room and make a pretty backdrop for the seating.

SOLUTION

- Hanem and Cameron already had new drywall up, so the first order of business was to lay new pre-finished hardwood flooring to unite the two areas.

- To enclose the stairs for safety, I added balusters and handrails. Simple, square balusters suit the style of the house and keep the feeling of openness between the living and dining areas.

- To maximize space and seating in the living area, I chose an armless, contemporary L-shaped sectional that tucks into the corner. A clean-lined, contemporary armchair balances it and rounds out the conversation group. With its exposed legs, the chair is less bulky and space-eating than a skirted chair would be.

- To make the little window seem larger without breaking the budget on fabric, I covered the window area with simple sheers. Banded linen panels hang at the sides, covering the wall for a soft, luxurious look.

- For much-needed storage and a fabulous focal point, I designed a space-saving floor-to-bulkhead cabinetry unit for one wall of the dining area. A beautiful, compact electric fireplace sits in the center of the unit so it's visible from the table. It adds ambience, elegance, and a little heat and needs nothing more than wiring for the plug.

- The old rooms had only a couple of bare bulbs. After upgrading the wiring, I brought in light where there once was darkness with a ceiling full of recessed fixtures, two contemporary cylinder sconces at the fireplace, a slick stainless-steel pendant over the dining table, and a table lamp in the living room.

RIGHT: An antique pine cabinet conceals the TV. The upholstered cube beside it serves as extra seating or can be pulled over to the sofa to serve as an ottoman.

STYLE ELEMENTS

- Because it's contrast, not color, that makes a small space feel even smaller, I chose a low-contrast color scheme of sage-olive for the walls and a soft cream for trim. Even though the color is fairly light, I tinted the primer with the paint color to give better coverage. This also shows up any imperfections in the drywall so they can be patched and sanded perfectly smooth before the paint goes on.

- Low-contrast fabrics—creamy beige upholstery and linen draperies with horizontal bands of pale tan and sage—create a quiet flow through both rooms. Nothing jumps out to stop your eye, so the space feels more expansive. To give the dining chairs a little visual interest, I upholstered them in two tones of beige.

- I anchored each seating group with a beautiful light-color area rug. A camel-color runner carpets the stairs to give the old wood a new look.

- Even small rooms need a teeny bit of contrast to keep them from feeling boring! I chose pre-finished flooring in a capital-G gorgeous dark-walnut stain to ground all the quiet tones. A similar dark-walnut stain on the fireplace cabinetry contrasts with the walls to emphasize the feature as the dining room's focal point.

ABOVE: An elevated fireplace brings loads of character and ambience to the dining room, and cabinets above and below provide lots of storage in a small space. Because this wall is shared with the neighbor, I installed an electric fireplace, which needs no flues or chimney. I paired Cameron's antique pine harvest table with contemporary upholstered dining chairs that can be moved into the living room when more seating is needed.

OPPOSITE: A big framed mirror is one of my favorite ways to expand space! A pair of pierced, illuminated columns adds an interesting architectural element as well as unexpected accent lighting.

Pillows stitched from pleated Ultrasuede and pleated silk break up the solid expanse of the sofa with soft color and interesting texture. Recessed fixtures around the perimeter of the room wash the walls with light, providing general illumination that's not harsh or glaring.

BELOW: Just inside the entry, I stole 9 inches of precious floor space for a closet that will hold coats, boots, and umbrellas. On the wall beside it, I hung one of the hockey pictures that Hanem collects.

2 RECIPES FOR COMPROMISE

SOMETHING FOR EVERYONE

CHALLENGE

Neil is the lone male in a family of females—even the dogs are girls! He has been retreating to the garage to watch sports on TV, but he'd really like to turn the family's basement into a sort of "man's pit." While Lolet is happy for him to come in from the cold, she wants a space the whole family can enjoy. That's where the tug-of-war over style begins. He likes dark, manly tones and modern lighting. She likes bright colors and a more feminine feel and is willing to offer a significant bribe—her famous Chicken Adobo—to fend off a moody, dimly lit pub look.

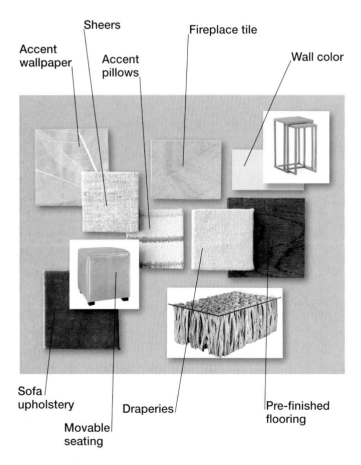

Sheers

Accent wallpaper

Accent pillows

Fireplace tile

Wall color

Sofa upholstery

Movable seating

Draperies

Pre-finished flooring

BEFORE: The only thing this basement had going for it (from Neil's point of view) was the TV! Overscaled, mismatched seating was badly worn, thanks to some help from the dogs, and the fireplace didn't work anymore. The dusty-rose carpet brought Lolet's favorite color downstairs—much to Neil's dismay.

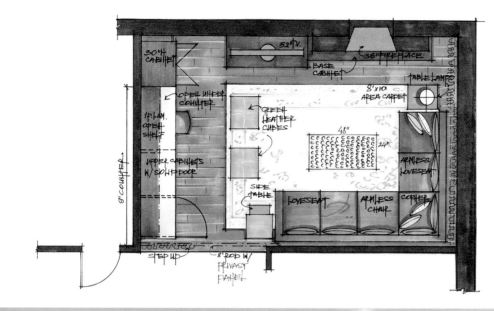

AFTER: The natural elements of beautiful sandstone tiles and dark-stained wood set a gender-neutral tone and create a warm, cozy background for ingredients that strike a balance between rustic-masculine and elegant-feminine. A sprawling sectional sofa covered in bark-brown velvet is pet- and kid-friendly. Leather-upholstered ottomans serve as more seating or can be moved closer to the sofa to support tired feet.

SOLUTION

- I started by tearing out the old bulky brick hearth, the nonfunctioning fireplace, the popcorn stucco ceiling, and the old rose carpet. In place of the carpet, I laid a beautiful pre-finished hardwood floor in a medium-tone cherry. It's durable, hard-wearing, and easy to clean, perfect for a room that will accommodate two dogs and a family of four.

- I divided the room into two zones, one that's all about function and one that focuses on relaxation and watching TV.

- To anchor the relaxation zone, I installed two sets of low custom cabinets. One is a base for a slim, gas-insert fireplace, and the other supports a big-screen television. Now the room has a decorative focal point and a functional focal point—and they're conveniently located side by side!

- A roomy L-shaped sectional and a pair of upholstered cubes provide plenty of comfortable seating in the TV zone.

- Along one end wall, I put in ready-to-assemble cabinetry for toy storage and office space. A bar fridge under the counter keeps beverages chilled and conveniently close for game days or movie nights.

- Because this was a basement with one tiny window and not much in the way of lighting, I installed lots of new recessed lights in the ceiling (no dimly lit pub here!). Under-cabinet fixtures over the desk use xenon bulbs, which stay cool—a real advantage when placed over a work surface. Sconces on the wall opposite the fireplace are installed a little lower than usual to frame the new seating and provide light for reading.

LEFT: A roomy L-shaped sectional provides plenty of seating for Neil and his wife, mother, daughter, and two dogs—or for Neil and his guy friends when they come over to watch TV. Covering the entire end wall with draperies creates the illusion of an above-ground window.

ABOVE: Handsome ready-to-assemble cabinets create a wall of function at one end of the room. The slab-front doors and sleek metal handles speak to Neil's preference for modern style, while the prominent wood grain brings in a rustic feel. The long counter accommodates a home office or can serve as a buffet for a party, and the under-counter fridge keeps beverages handy.

ABOVE: A stunning sandstone-tile fireplace surround stretches all the way to the ceiling. The tile is set close without grout to take advantage of the pattern, which gives the effect of wood grain. Custom storage doubles as a hearth, and a matching unit provides media storage and a base for the big-screen TV—an absolute must-have for any "man's pit"!

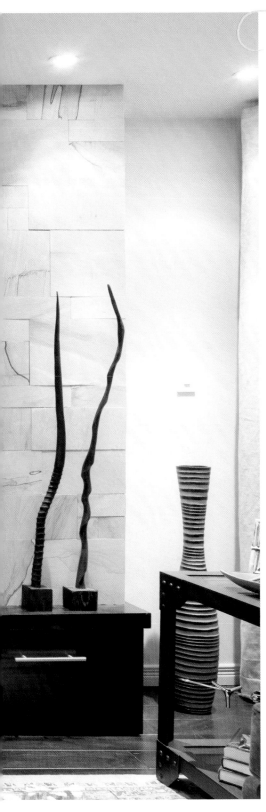

STYLE ELEMENTS

- A nature-inspired color scheme is gender-neutral, and I found a fabulous wallpaper that kicks everything off. It incorporates real skeletonized leaves in a random pattern and brings a punch of color to the accent wall.

- The creamy tone in the leaf veins led me to a cream-color countertop for the desk and storage area.

- Picking up on the wallpaper's green background, I chose a beautiful green linen brocade for the drapery panels. They frame an expanse of natural linen that covers the entire window wall, creating the illusion of an above-ground window and adding feminine softness to the room.

- For the fireplace, I chose a 12 x 24-inch sandstone tile with a subtle, random pattern that looks like wood grain. It's rustic and manly and picks up on the walnut tones of the cabinetry and the warm medium brown of the floor.

- A durable, kid-friendly, 100-percent polyester in bark brown covers the sectional. It matches the color of the dogs too, so this is one sectional that says "Pets Welcome!" Pillows in a range of textures from coarse and nubby to velvety-soft break up the expanse of solid color.

- When I choose a wall color, I think about what will be in front of it. I want the sectional to contrast with the walls and the sandstone tile and draperies to blend in, so a light almond is the perfect choice.

RIGHT: A tall cabinet organizes toys now and can accommodate files, office supplies, or games as the family's needs change.

LEFT: An absolutely perfect coffee table marries rustic and modern materials, with tightly packed branches topped by glass. Chrome sconces and furnishings with clean, straight lines speak to Neil's modern tastes, while luscious, touchable fabrics address Lolet's feminine sensibilities.

BELOW: Using this fabulous (but expensive) wallpaper on an accent wall brings in a punch of color and pattern without breaking the budget. Cool-burning xenon bulbs installed under the shelf cast bright light down on the desk surface for excellent visibility.

COMFORTABLE COMPROMISE

CHALLENGE

Allison is a financial analyst who loves urban life and hip, downtown style. Garren owns a woodworking and guitar business and loves the outdoors as well as hunting for bargains at garage sales. Their new family room is furnished with some of his old finds, including a beanbag chair and sofas upholstered in a 1980s print. Allison is desperate to update the room but can't decide what she wants. Garren is no help, because he's fine with things the way they are. The only thing the couple agreed on was to call on me to arbitrate!

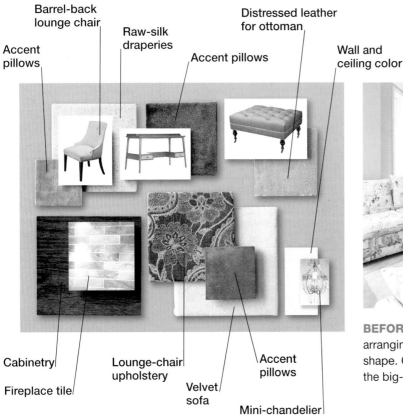

Barrel-back lounge chair
Accent pillows
Raw-silk draperies
Accent pillows
Distressed leather for ottoman
Wall and ceiling color
Cabinetry
Fireplace tile
Lounge-chair upholstery
Velvet sofa
Mini-chandelier
Accent pillows

BEFORE: Outdated sofas were not at all to Allison's taste, and arranging furniture was a challenge because of the room's odd shape. Garren had installed a fireplace, but it was no match for the big-screen television as a focal point.

AFTER: Repositioning the fireplace so it's in the center of the wall and surrounding it with rugged slate tile immediately gives the room a focus. Beside it, a new built-in media cabinet balances the scale of the TV and incorporates it into the architecture, much to Garren's satisfaction. New seating is contemporary and comfortable, just the way Allison likes it.

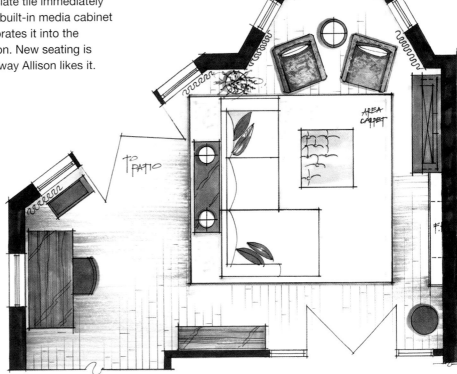

SOLUTION

- Designing this large room was complicated by the fact that a traffic path to the backyard had to be kept clear. I resolved the issue by making the fireplace wall the focus and anchoring the main seating to it.

- Garren's beanbag chair and 1980s sofas had to go! In their place, I brought in a big L-shaped sectional with a chaise component to divide the lounging area from the traffic path. A pair of lounge chairs nestles just inside the bay window, giving that area a function while still putting the chairs inside the conversation zone.

- To give the fireplace its due as a focal point, I built out the wall and repositioned the insert in the center. Then I surrounded it with large-format, rugged slate tile for lots of he-man texture.

- Custom cabinetry beside the fireplace incorporates the big-screen TV so it's in proper scale with the room.

- The room has plenty of natural light, but for nighttime lighting I installed monopoint spotlights on the I-beam and recessed lights elsewhere in the ceiling.

RIGHT: The wall beside the doors to the patio offers the perfect spot for a desk that can double as a buffet when the couple entertains. Creating this little secondary work space takes advantage of an empty corner and helps bring the room into balance.

BELOW: A big, super-inviting sectional defines the lounging and conversation zone. The flat, tailored arms and clean, straight lines are contemporary enough for Allison. The deep seat and plump cushions are comfy enough for Garren.

ABOVE: The focal-point wall sums up this marriage of opposites: Rugged tile and warm wood have a masculine feel, but the installation is linear and contemporary. The television screen angles down for better viewing if necessary.

STYLE ELEMENTS

- Arbitrating between Allison's and Garren's contrasting styles meant juggling a whole bunch of opposites. The large-format slate tile was my jumping-off point. Its rugged texture speaks to Garren's rustic, outdoorsy tastes, but the installation is very contemporary and controlled, creating a linear pattern that addresses Allison's contemporary style.

- To correspond to the linear effect of the surround, I designed the media cabinetry with the wood grain running horizontally as well. This application appeals to the woodworker in Garren, and the slab-front doors and square pulls are right up Allison's alley.

- The room's color palette of taupe, bark, and rust came straight from the slate. A creamy taupe velvet covers the sectional, and a luscious paisley in browns, rusts, and creams covers the lounge chairs.

- To play up the stone and wood, I painted the walls a quiet cream color and the ceilings white.

- To contrast with the contemporary seating, I chose a traditional ottoman upholstered in distressed butterscotch leather. It has a men's-club feel for Garren, but the large scale gives it a contemporary twist.

- To make the most of the beautiful view outdoors, I devised a window treatment that's a little bit rustic and a little bit elegant. Woven-grass blinds installed inside the window frames bring in natural texture. They're unlined, so they diffuse light rather than block it. For refinement and softness, I framed the bay and the doors with raw-silk draperies. Goblet pleats in the headers are more tailored and structured than pinch pleats; a little roll of cardboard slips inside each pleat to make it hold its shape. In a nod to Garren, the draperies hang on hand-wrought, antique iron rods installed just below the crown molding.

LEFT: Luscious linen-look raw-silk draperies fall in soft columns, framing the bay. A sparkly chandelier is a little feminine touch for Allison that contrasts with the natural texture of woven-grass blinds for Garren.

Seating divides the big, oddly shaped room into logical zones, with the desk area on one side of the path to the double doors and the sectional on the other. A beautiful patterned area rug helps define the TV-and-relaxation zone.

POLAR OPPOSITES

CHALLENGE

Ken and Sue are a textbook example of the old saying, "Opposites attract." He's a solitary guy who loves to read and play his guitar. For Sue, life is a dinner party, and her philosophy is the more, the merrier. Their opinions on design are just as polarized. She likes neutrals and sleek, contemporary style, while he prefers color, antiques, and a sense of tradition. They work at home in separate offices, but the open-concept living-dining room is where they relax together at the end of the day, and they'd like it to be comfortable for both of them. Can I arrange this marriage of tastes? Yes, I can!

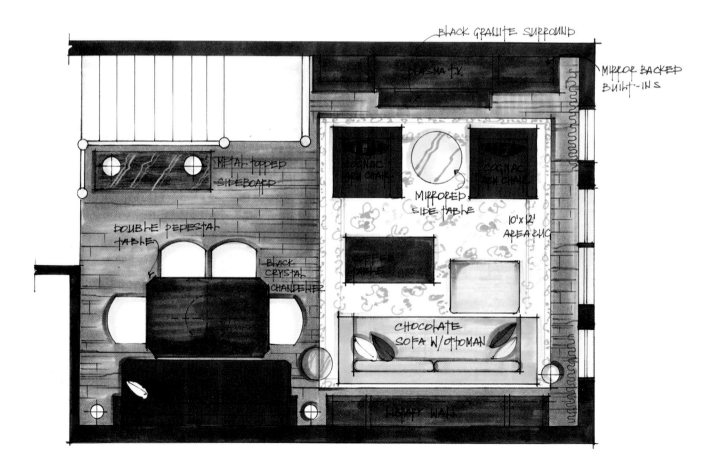

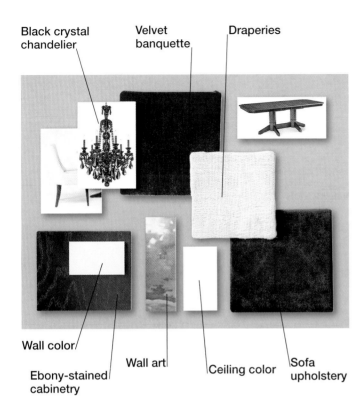

Black crystal chandelier
Velvet banquette
Draperies
Wall color
Ebony-stained cabinetry
Wall art
Ceiling color
Sofa upholstery

BEFORE: Sue bought the house before she met Ken, so the basically beige living–dining room reflected her preference for neutral colors and modern design. Unfortunately, the room didn't address Ken's love of color and antiques at all.

AFTER: The new space is all about comfort, color, and compromise. A dramatic, antique-velvet banquette and black crystal chandelier nod to Ken's traditional tastes, while upholstered furniture with clean lines and simple shapes speak to Sue's modern sensibilities.

SOLUTION

- The room already had good bones, but the space wasn't as functional as it could be. I used the existing bulkheads and columns as frames for a full-height banquette in the dining room and new custom-built bookcases in the living room. Custom woodwork enhances the existing architecture, framing in the niches and giving them new purpose.

- The banquette anchors the dining area, which can now accommodate both everyday meals and Sue's famous dinner parties. I replaced her old glass dining table with a wooden rectangular one that has extra leaves stored under the top, so it can expand to seat 10.

- In the living room, the built-in bookcases offer lots of display space for Ken's books and collections. A long shelf bridges them to serve as a sofa table and provide for more display.

- The old fireplace was fine, but it needed a facelift for a more modern look. A shiny black granite surround, very cool and contemporary, gives it a real "wow" factor. I hung a flat-screen TV above the fireplace to save space and combine the room's two natural focal points.

- Beside the fireplace, there were two empty recesses just crying out for cabinetry. So I gave it to them! Cabinets with display shelves above and storage below give once-wasted space a purpose. Mirrors on the backs of the cabinets help expand the sense of space.

- A pair of comfy lounge chairs opposite a large, luxurious sofa meets Ken's need for a place to read and Sue's desire for more seating for guests.

- To update and soften the windows, I took down the shutters and united the windows with privacy sheers and drapery panels in light, soft linen.

ABOVE: Because the banquette is the first thing you see when you walk in, I super-sized it to make a dramatic style statement. The button-tufted back in henna velvet is rich and traditional for Ken, but the scale makes it modern. Clean, white walls and contrasting dark woodwork also give the space a modern vibe for Sue.

BELOW: The banquette turns a wasted niche into functional, club-like seating and allows room for a larger, longer table and comfortable chairs. New upholstered chairs in the living area pick up the color of the banquette, unifying the two spaces visually.

STYLE ELEMENTS

- The marriage of opposites really starts with a gorgeous crystal chandelier for the dining room. The shape references a historical style, but the black crystals give it a modern look.

- The new banquette also combines contrasting styles, joining traditional button-tufted detailing with dramatic scale for a look that's both rooted in history and up-to-date.

- Because Sue suffers from color-phobia, I kept the walls and main furniture pieces neutral. Crisp white walls and ebony-stained cabinetry create a high-contrast, modern background for a chocolate velvet sofa, creamy upholstered dining chairs, and snowy white draperies and sheers. Splashes of color—in the banquette and two lounge chairs—speak back and forth between the dining and living room but don't fight with each other. And against the neutral backdrop, a little color goes a long way in shaping the look of the space.

- To pull the living room together, I laid down a beautiful area rug in beige, tan, and paprika. It adds a touch of pattern to contrast with all the solid colors.

- In addition to recessed ceiling lights for overall illumination, I installed puck lights in the cabinetry to highlight displays. Sleek, contemporary sconces of Lucite and polished chrome play off the chandelier and bring in the contemporary look Sue loves (see page 71).

RIGHT: Custom-built ebony cabinetry puts wasted space to work on both sides of the living room. A long, chocolate velvet sofa and cushy velvet upholstered chairs face off over the perfect coffee table. It has a cool, contemporary bronze finish and traditional graceful cabriole legs—a little something for Sue, a little something for Ken.

LEFT: Mirror backing in the cabinetry reflects light and expands the sense of space in the living room. Glass shelves keep the look open and clean. The black quartz fireplace surround picks up on the black crystal chandelier in the dining room, helping to tie the two spaces together.

BELOW: Sleek ebony bookcases are contemporary for her and store lots of books for him. Puck lights accent the wall art and sofa table display. Accent pillows play off the neutral scheme and add texture and pattern.

URBAN COUNTRY

CHALLENGE

Barry and Beverly are small-town folks who have moved to a charming 1910 row house in the big city. There's just one small problem: The furniture from their old house really isn't working here. The overstuffed furniture is too big and a little too "country" for the new place, and the assortment of bookcases they've accumulated to display all their books and collections looks chaotic instead of organized. They'd like to hold on to their country roots but move toward a more sophisticated look better suited to the urban setting.

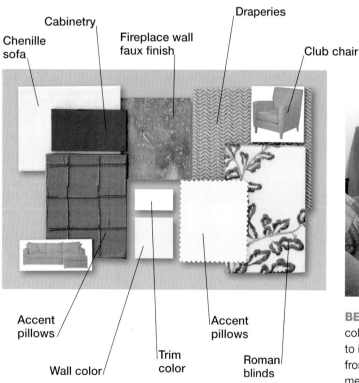

Chenille sofa • Cabinetry • Fireplace wall faux finish • Draperies • Club chair • Accent pillows • Wall color • Trim color • Accent pillows • Roman blinds

BEFORE: With oversized, country-style furniture and a motley collection of bookcases, this cozy row house wasn't living up to its potential. Another problem: The dining area was farther from the kitchen than the living room, which made serving meals something of a marathon.

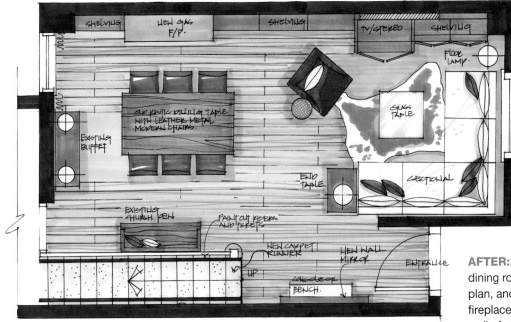

AFTER: Flipping the living room and dining room creates a more logical floor plan, and tearing out the old decorative fireplace makes room for a fabulous wall of storage to replace the assorted bookcases. A new fireplace set into a gorgeous faux-finished wall creates a stunning focal point for the dining area.

ABOVE: A faux-rusted-metal wall pays homage to Barry and Beverly's country roots, while the sleek new fireplace and chocolate-color slab shelving introduce the look of urban chic they want to incorporate.

SOLUTION

- Before tackling the "big-city makeover," I addressed the issue of room layout. Having to walk through the living room to get from the kitchen to the dining area made no sense, so I simply swapped the two for much better function.

- The old decorative fireplace was oddly placed and didn't really serve as a focal point for either the living room or the dining room. I ripped it out and put in a long, super-flexible, custom-designed storage system to organize absolutely everything. Thick slab shelves snap into grooves and are hefty enough to make an architectural statement. A deep cabinet at the living room end holds the TV, with closed storage below.

- In the new dining area, I built out the wall to accommodate a combination electric-gas fireplace. It's raised above table height so that it's visible from the dining table as well as from the living room.

- To better suit the scale of the skinny row house, I brought in new furniture that leans to the warm, casual, comfortable side of contemporary style. An armless, three-piece L-shaped sectional fits perfectly into the 10 x 7-foot living room, with enough space left over for a small club chair and footstool. In the dining room, a wooden trestle table and sleek, modern chairs provide maximum function in a minimum of space.

ABOVE: A gorgeous new "great wall of storage" runs along one wall, tying the dining room and living room together. In the living room, the cabinetry includes a media center. An L-shaped sectional and a small-scale club chair are the perfect seating solution for the small space.

STYLE ELEMENTS

- The original hardwood floors were in beautiful shape and supplied lots of vintage character. I painted the walls a soft putty color and the baseboards and crown moldings a crisp white to update the look.

- A chocolate finish for the storage system contrasts with the putty walls and anchors the room in a warm, modern style.

- The raised fireplace is the focal point for the dining room, but the subtle faux-rust finish is the real story, a country reference that complements the sleek and contemporary fireplace. It starts with a coat of copper oil-based paint, followed by a red glaze and spatters of rusty brown that are mottled and rubbed to blend them in. Then the wet paint is sprayed lightly with paint thinner and worked with a fluffy, square, bristle brush until the desired effect is achieved.

- The faux finish inspired a warm, rich palette of fabrics in rust, wheat, and earthy browns. A wheat-color chenille on the sectional opens up the sense of space in the living area, and the paprika-color armchair and ottoman pull the color of the accent wall over to that end of the room.

- For the window treatments, I found a gorgeous embroidered sheer to use as Roman blinds. The floral is a little traditional, but stylized for a city feel. Because the fabric is so delicate, I lined the blinds to bring out the pattern. In the dining room, I flanked the Roman blind with long herringbone-silk drapery panels, to give some mass and volume to the window. I used the same silk for a curtain to draw across the doorway between the kitchen and the dining area, for those times when Beverly wants to hide the after-dinner mess and just enjoy her guests.

- The rooms needed all-new lighting, so I chose a vintage-inspired forged-iron alabaster pendant for the living room to pay homage to the age of the house. In the dining room, I installed a fixture that goes beyond sleek and urban-cool: It's like a piece of art, with flowers and tiny leaves on a super-stylized branch. Gorgeous!

LEFT: As much an art statement as a light source, this unique fixture features LED bulbs sparkling inside tiny crystal flowers. Crystal leaves dangle from the stylized branch.

ABOVE: Urban meets country in the dining area, where contemporary black leather dining chairs pull up to a wooden dining table that combines a clean-lined slab top with shaped, traditional-style trestle legs. Silk draperies frame the window and draw across the doorway that leads to the kitchen. A beautiful area rug brings the color of the faux-rust wall down to the floor.

ABOVE: Rust, floral, and tan pillows break up the expanse of solid color on the sectional. In such a small room, plug-in wall-mounted sconces eliminate the need for side tables and provide task lighting for the sofa. A clear acrylic coffee table also helps open up the room because it takes up no space visually.

BELOW: In the living room, the media center is deeper than the shelves on each side not only to accommodate the TV but also to balance the fireplace at the other end of the room.

A MULTIFUNCTIONAL SPACE FOR TWO

CHALLENGE

David and Daniela have already bought their first home, an 800-square-foot loft in a hip downtown setting, but Daniela isn't moving in until after the wedding. Right now the loft looks like the typical post-college bachelor pad, complete with futon and ratty recliner. Daniela has something much more sophisticated and urban-hip in mind. This pre-wedding makeover is about more than style, however. The loft's main area has to multitask as a living room, dining room, multimedia room, storage area, and home office. Fortunately, I have my bag of Ingenious Small-Space Tricks with me!

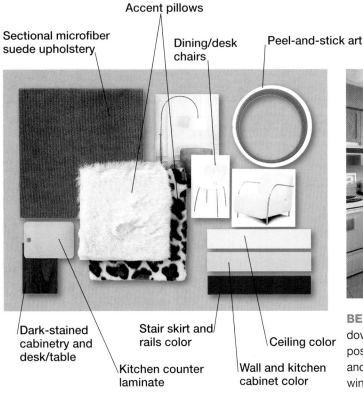

Sectional microfiber suede upholstery

Accent pillows

Dining/desk chairs

Peel-and-stick art

Dark-stained cabinetry and desk/table

Stair skirt and rails color

Kitchen counter laminate

Ceiling color

Wall and kitchen cabinet color

BEFORE: The bachelor-pad days are numbered for this small downtown loft. Sparsely furnished with the bare necessities for post-college life, it needs a swift makeover to become David and Daniela's new matrimonial home. And those blinds on the windows have to go!

AFTER: Cool color unifies the entire space, and a long L-shaped sectional anchors the living area. Two sets of fabric shades control light at the tall windows; the upper set can be raised and lowered by remote control, and the lower set is operated manually.

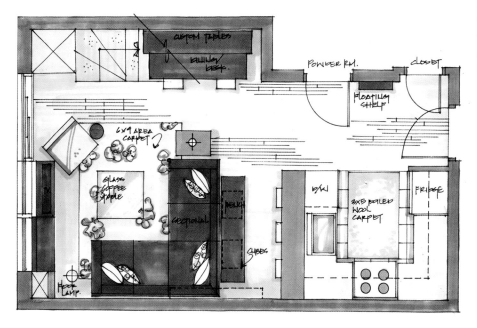

ABOVE: Painting the kitchen cabinets to blend with the walls makes the whole space feel larger. The stainless-steel-and-glass coffee table and side table are not only sophisticated and contemporary, they also take up little space visually. Nesting side tables can also serve as guest seating.

SOLUTION

- First small-space trick: Unify all of the walls and vertical surfaces with color, so there's nothing to stop the eye. That means this makeover actually starts with the kitchen, a little wedding present from me to Daniela and David. I painted the cabinets and all of the walls the same cool neutral color, which automatically makes the space feel larger.

- Second small-space trick: Keep the contrast low. New laminate counters that look just like stainless steel (but cost a fraction of the price) blend with the cabinets and help make the kitchen flow right into the new living space. For the icing on the cake, I installed a mirrored backsplash. It grabs light from the windows and brings it all the way into the interior of the loft. (That's my third small-space trick!)

- In place of the recliner and futon, I put in a long L-shaped sectional that defines the living area and will seat many, many friends or just Daniela and David. The TV sits in front of the window, where there will be no glare, on a custom-built open-storage unit.

- I gave the niche under the stairs a whole new function as a home-office zone. Here's where I used one of my truly ingenious space-saving, multitasking solutions: a computer desk that rolls out to serve as a dining table for two or eight! Nesting tables beside the sofa do double duty as dining seats for guests.

- The 17-foot-high windows let in tons of gorgeous daylight, but they face south, so the loft can get pretty warm. In place of the tattered blinds and tangle of cords, I covered the windows with a UV-filtering film, then installed a two-tiered system of fabric shades. The upper shades can be raised and lowered by remote control and the lower ones by hand.

RIGHT: A long, low custom-built storage unit puts the TV at a convenient height for viewing. Fabric shades screen the light and soften the architecture without being too fussy.

83

STYLE ELEMENTS

- A hip, urban kitchen means stainless steel, so that was my jumping-off point for color for the whole loft. I chose a steely blue for all of the walls and kitchen cabinets and soft blue fabric for the window shades. Charcoal gray paint for the stairs grounds the scheme.

- I upholstered the sectional in a very tactile, super-durable mink-color microfiber suede. It's a good, basic neutral color that they can work around, using different fabrics and accessories as their tastes change.

- To break up the expanse of solid color on the sofa, I added fun and funky accent pillows stitched from leopard fabric (for him), soft, fluffy, white faux mink (for her), a shaved polar bear faux fur, and a fun organic pattern in a color I call "bridesmaid's blue."

- To balance the cool, steely hues, I used warm, dark-stained wood for the computer desk, dining table, TV stand, and storage and display units. Clean, straight lines give these pieces a very modern look, to suit Daniela's tastes, and they also enhance the streamlined, open feeling that a small space needs.

- The only thing David really wanted to keep (besides the TV) was his collection of toy cars. I designed a pair of long, skinny, mirror-backed display boxes that not only spotlight his cars with puck lights but also enhance the illusion of space by reflecting light and views back into the room.

- Since David and Daniela are just starting out, they don't have much in the way of art to dress up the walls. For the high wall adjacent to the windows, I wallpapered a series of panels, framed them, and hung them to serve as instant art.

- Very cool, industrial-style track lights and pendants replace the dinky globe fixture in the kitchen, and under-cabinet lights provide task lighting over the counters. Above the sectional, another row of track lights provides overall lighting, supplemented by a swooping floor lamp and a table lamp in the living area.

LEFT: Long display boxes fitted with puck lights and mirror backing showcase David's toy cars. The mirror also helps bounce light back into the room and adds an illusion of depth.

ABOVE: In the under-stairs home office, a custom-built slab-style desk holds the monitor and hard drive, and a table on wheels fits under it to hold the keyboard. When guests come for dinner, the table can be rolled out and pulled up to the sofa; the desk chairs become guest seating. Peel-and-stick circles applied to the adjacent wall add a little artistic interest!

BELOW: Ordinary faux-wood cabinets got a fresh facelift with paint and deluxe glass knobs. Stainless-steel laminate countertops are so convincing, you can't tell they're not the real thing (see how they blend right in with the stainless-steel sink?). I covered the old countertop with dark-stained wood to match the custom storage and display pieces.

ABOVE: A faux cowhide rug puts a little funky pattern on the floor, and a framed, wallpapered board puts pattern on the wall. The swooping floor lamp is a good way to bring light into the center of a room when the ceiling is so high that pendant fixtures would be difficult to install.

VENUS AND MARS

CHALLENGE

Stella works in the world of high fashion, while Chris lives, eats, and breathes sports, and the big, sunny, family room in their new home doesn't really please either of them. It's boring and bland, with a mishmash of dated furnishings gathered around a big-screen TV. Stella would like the room to be stylish yet comfortable, a place to gather with girlfriends and talk. Chris just wants an even bigger television, so that when they host parties for championship sports events, everyone has a good view. My challenge is to turn this style-starved space into a room that's fit for both Girls' Night and Sports Night.

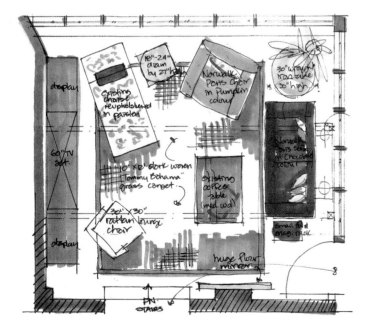

BEFORE: Mismatched furniture that they each brought into the marriage circles around a big flat-screen TV that is too small to suit Chris. The only two pieces they'd really like to keep are the coffee table, which they just bought, and the chaise, which is an antique psychiatrist's couch Chris inherited from his grandmother.

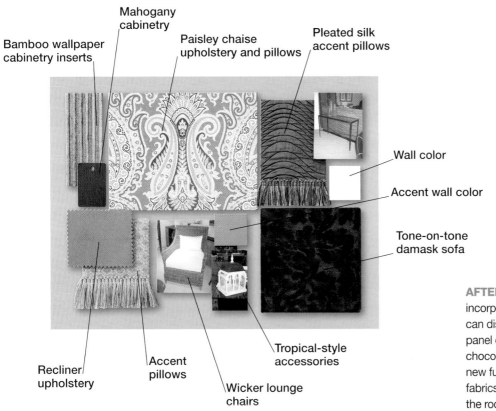

Bamboo wallpaper cabinetry inserts

Mahogany cabinetry

Paisley chaise upholstery and pillows

Pleated silk accent pillows

Wall color

Accent wall color

Tone-on-tone damask sofa

Recliner upholstery

Accent pillows

Wicker lounge chairs

Tropical-style accessories

AFTER: A gorgeous new wall of storage incorporates a huge flat-screen TV that can disappear behind bamboo-and-reed panel doors when it's Girls' Night. A rich chocolate-color area rug anchors stylish new furniture upholstered in lush, plush fabrics and warm, cozy colors that make the room inviting for the girls and the boys.

SOLUTION

- The focal point of the room for Chris will be a television the size of a small country! But to keep Stella happy, it needs to disappear when it's not in use. To satisfy both, I designed a custom cabinet that fills one wall—that's 12 feet of cabinetry reaching 7 feet high! A new 60-inch flat-screen TV occupies the center section. Sliding doors on an industrial track roll back to reveal the television and close to show off display shelves on either side.

- The bones of the room were fine, so creating a sumptuous setting depended on furniture and color. In addition to reupholstering the antique chaise, I brought in a new sofa and side chair, and just for Chris, a comfy recliner that hides its kick-back identity under a super-stylish retro club-chair look.

- The creamy walls and light-wheat carpet were in good shape, but the room needed a little spicy heat. I kicked things up a notch with one accent wall in a hot burnt-orange. Because intense colors such as red and orange can be tricky to apply, I tinted the primer with a little black paint. The deep base allows you to get good, solid paint coverage without having to apply about a million coats!

- To make the most of the indoor-outdoor connection that all those windows offered, I replaced the old paper blinds with simple wood ones lined with blackout lining. The clean lines play up the architecture, and the natural texture speaks to the exotic look I wanted.

- Although the room had plenty of natural light by day, the existing fixtures weren't up to the job at night. I used the two junction boxes to run 8-foot-long tracks along the back of the beams, where they would be hidden. Wired to a dimmer switch, the positionable fixtures can be directed where needed for reading or general illumination.

RIGHT: A fabulous custom cabinet marries the couple's Venus-and-Mars interests. Slide the doors to the sides, and the TV is revealed. Push them to the center, and sandblasted glass shelves display Stella's fashionable collections. Cabinets and drawers below provide tons of storage.

STYLE ELEMENTS

- To give the cabinetry an exotic, tropical-island look, I chose dark wood for the frame and dressed up the doors and backs of the display cabinets with wallpaper inserts of bamboo and reed. I also had the glass shelves sandblasted to add some texture and to diffuse the accent lighting installed in the top of the cabinet.

- The lush, plush scheme really came to life with rich and decadent fabrics. A beautiful paisley for the 7-foot-long chaise and some throw pillows inspired the tone-on-tone chocolate damask on the sofa and the suede-like paprika-orange upholstery on the recliner.

- A chocolate rug layered over the existing wall-to-wall carpet anchors the seating group and makes the fabric colors pop.

LEFT: One spicy-hot accent wall kicks out the old blah, too-beige feeling and nods to Stella's fashion-forward sense of style. A huge framed mirror bounces back light and views and expands the sense of space.

ABOVE: Wood blinds, a wicker chair, and a beautiful paisley print set the tone for a feeling of exotic luxury. The warm, spicy color scheme is manly enough to suit Chris and his friends, but rich and cozy enough to make Stella and her friends feel at home.

RIGHT: It's a game of conceal and reveal. Stella really didn't want the television to dominate the room, so the bamboo-and-reed-covered doors slide to the center to reveal dramatically lit display shelves.

LEFT: Chris wanted a television big enough that a roomful of sports fans could all watch the game together. Slide the doors to the sides, and voilà! A glorious piece of technology takes center stage.

FROM FRAT-GUY FRUMPY TO FEMALE-FRIENDLY

CHALLENGE

Patricia and Manny are about to get married, and they've already bought their first home together, a beautiful 1920s house with loads of architectural character. Patricia isn't moving in until after the wedding, but Manny and the dogs have made themselves at home—and frankly, it's kind of a masculine mess. A beer keg, mini-fridge, video games, samurai swords, and a giant TV fill up one end of the main room, and a frumpy sofa sits way over on the other side. Patricia wants to see some major changes before she lets Manny carry her over the threshold!

Modern/rustic coffee table

Existing woodwork

Wall color

Crown molding color

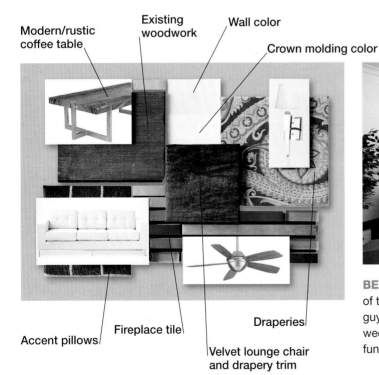

Accent pillows

Fireplace tile

Velvet lounge chair and drapery trim

Draperies

BEFORE: Manny and Patricia loved the architectural character of their home, but Patricia wasn't too thrilled with Manny's frat-guy sense of style. She wouldn't be moving in until after their wedding, but she wanted to come home to a sophisticated, functional, and female-friendly living room—and this wasn't it!

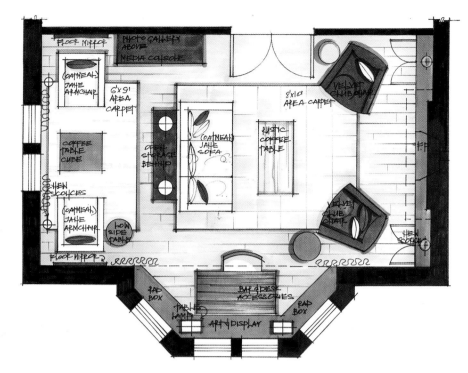

The floor plan is labeled with the following annotations:

FLOOR MIRROR
PHOTO GALLERY ABOVE
MEDIA CONSOLE
(OATMEAL) JANE ARMCHAIR
6'x9' AREA CARPET
8'x10' AREA CARPET
VELVET OTTOMAN
COFFEE TABLE CUBE
OPEN STORAGE BEHIND
(OATMEAL) JANE SOFA
RUSTIC COFFEE TABLE
OPEN SCONCES
(OATMEAL) JANE ARMCHAIR
LOW SIDE TABLE
VELVET CLUB CHAIR
OPEN SCONCES
FLOOR MIRROR
RAD BOX
TABLE LAMP
BAR & DESK ACCESSORIES
RAD BOX
ART & DISPLAY

AFTER: Warm, neutral tones have a masculine feel, and beautiful paisley draperies soften the look with a feminine touch. Contemporary furnishings are sophisticated but comfortable, and three zones—conversation, home office, and library—pack more function into the main living area. Modern elements Patricia will love complement the vintage character of the original woodwork.

I enhanced the beautiful fireplace and built-in bookcases with a new tile surround and hearth and built out the wall above to hold a new flat-screen TV. Positioning the sofa closer to the fireplace opens up space behind it for a cozy library zone. Luxurious paisley draperies frame the bay window and create the sense of a new room-within-a-room.

SOLUTION

- Patricia and Manny both loved the room's architectural features, so I kept the bones of the room intact and used the architecture as a starting point to create a space they both could enjoy.

- I started by dividing the room into zones: a TV and conversation zone centered on the fireplace, a home office tucked into the big bay window, and an intimate library zone at the end of the room opposite the fireplace.

- The bay window with its radiator is the first thing you see when you enter the room. Patricia wasn't crazy about the way it looked, so I covered it with a custom-built box that disguises the radiator while allowing the heat to escape. It's a perfect example of my design philosophy: If you can't beat it, join it! Deep, matching bookshelves fill the space under the windows on each side, turning the bay into something special, a cozy home office.

- Manny loves the mantel and woodwork, so I'm going to paint it all pink! Just kidding. Since he wasn't all that fond of the tile on the fireplace, I updated the look with a sleek, linear tile and covered the old hearth with a new porcelain tile. The new material goes right over the old after the surface has been scored to give it more "tooth." Resurfacing is almost as messy as starting from scratch, but what's a little mess when you've got a wedding looming?

- To eliminate the bulky, space-eating television and media equipment, I built out the wall above the fireplace and created a niche for a new flat-screen TV. Now the room's focal points— fireplace and television—are united in one eye-catching feature.

- To show off the beautiful woodwork around the windows, I hung woven wood blinds inside the frames. On a sheerness scale of one to five, these blinds are a two, so they filter light without entirely blocking it. Soft, sumptuous draperies frame the windows in the library and hang outside the bay to suggest a feeling of privacy.

- Manny loves the detail on the ceiling so we couldn't install recessed lights, but I had something better in mind—sconces. I replaced the old ones above the built-in bookcases and another pair on the opposite wall with cleaner, more contemporary ones to cast mood-setting light in each area.

RIGHT: The new radiator box and shelving blend right in with the original woodwork, as if they've been there forever. The bay window is the perfect spot for a desk and a pair of sleek lamps.

BELOW: A warm and cozy mix of rustic and refined creates a comfortable but sophisticated room for relaxing and entertaining. Metallic tones in the tile and sconces nod (distantly) to Manny's old stainless-steel beer fridge, and one of his samurai swords occupies center stage on the mantel. The television no longer dominates, set into the wall above the fireplace.

ABOVE: Gorgeous paisley draperies banded with deep chocolate hems hang from just below the crown molding to emphasize the room's beautiful high ceiling. Comfy modern club chairs covered in oatmeal tweed carve out an inviting spot for reading.

STYLE ELEMENTS

- The warmth and character of the original woodwork was the jumping-off point for the whole design. I found a luscious paisley fabric that would be the key to the feminine feel. Because it picks up the warm wood tones, it also inspires a masculine color palette of chocolatey brown, oatmeal, and caramel for the seating and accessories.

- A fresh coat of white paint highlights the woodwork and makes a clean background for the warm, neutral palette.

- Both Patricia and Manny grew up in houses where the living room was off-limits, and they want their living room to be a place where people feel comfortable sitting on the furniture. To please Patricia's sophisticated, modern taste, I chose a contemporary three-seater sofa and matching club chairs with clean lines and stainless-steel legs. An updated interpretation of traditional button tufting references the vintage character of the house.

- Next to the fireplace, I placed two irresistibly cozy (and manly) lounge chairs in the most perfect chocolate-brown velvet. It picks up on the paisley— and I hope it matches the dogs!

- To update the fireplace, I found a beautiful linear tile in a mix of metallic tones of bronze, stainless steel, brass, and copper. The metallics blend with the color of the wood and pick up on the stainless-steel legs of the furniture and the chrome bases of the new sconces. Charcoal porcelain tiles for the hearth relate to the darker tones in the fireplace tile.

- The draperies have a deep brown hem that aligns with the windowsills to create a uniform line that emphasizes the windows. The deep band of dark color also suggests a kind of base for the columns of fabric and gives them greater weight and impact. The blinds introduce varying tones to play off the wood tones, adding textural interest to the neutral scheme.

- Two yummy area rugs ground the main zones: an oatmeal-color geometric in the TV zone and a gorgeous Persian in the library zone. A long shelving unit backs up to the sofa to double as a console table and bookcase, and oversized framed mirrors lean against the walls to reflect light and views.

- For a totally personalized wall display, I hung a collage of Patricia's photography, using a terrific photo display system that makes putting up pictures a snap.

BELOW: Button tufting is traditional but tailored, an ideal accent for a streamlined, contemporary sofa. Metallic touches throughout the room—the sofa's stainless-steel frame and legs, the coffee table, table lamps, and sconces—balance the room's warm woods and vintage architecture for a perfect marriage of modern and traditional styles.

3

ALL IN THE FAMILY

A ROOM FOR YIAYIA

CHALLENGE

Super-busy mom Marie and her husband, Alex, just finished renovating most of their house. The only room left to tackle is the basement, which they want to fix up as a suite for Marie's mother, Sandra (better known as Yiayia—that's Greek for grandmother). They painted most of the walls with leftover blue paint from the kids' rooms, but it's a little too intense for Yiayia, and the countertop for the kitchenette cabinets overlaps the drawers so they can't open. Yiayia spends weeks at a time with the family, enjoying her grandchildren, and Marie wants the suite to be elegant, feminine, and special—just like her mother.

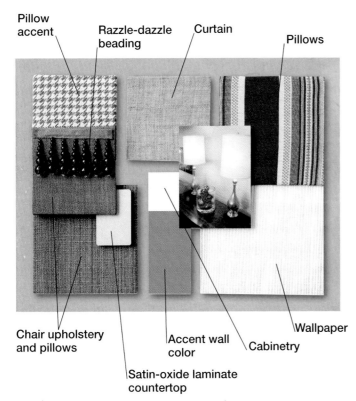

Pillow accent · Razzle-dazzle beading · Curtain · Pillows · Chair upholstery and pillows · Accent wall color · Satin-oxide laminate countertop · Cabinetry · Wallpaper

BEFORE: Marie and Alex started on the basement, painting most of the walls with leftover blue paint and installing some builders' floor model cabinets for a tiny kitchen. The only source of natural light is the window in the back door, and the ceiling is low—5 feet, 11 inches at the bulkhead!

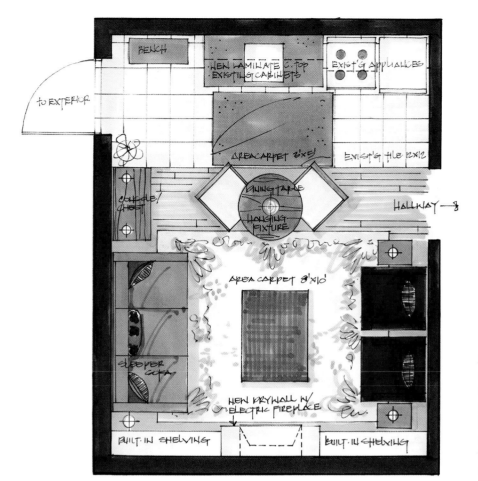

Labels within floor plan:
BENCH

NEW LAMINATE C. TOP
EXISTING CABINETS

EXIST'G APPLIANCES

to EXTERIOR

AREA CARPET 2'x6'

EXIST'G TILE 12x12

CONSOLE / CHEST

DINING TABLE

HANGING FIXTURE

HALLWAY →

AREA CARPET 8'x10'

SLEEPER SOFA

NEW DRYWALL W/ ELECTRIC FIREPLACE

BUILT-IN SHELVING

BUILT-IN SHELVING

AFTER: Metallic-backed grass cloth wallpaper opens up the small room with shimmer, shine, and light-reflecting color. Interior cabinet lighting and frosted-glass doors in the kitchenette add to the open feeling, and small-scale furniture is cozy, comfortable, and just right for the space.

SOLUTION

- Marie and Alex had already purchased pre-finished maple flooring but hadn't installed it yet—so I did!

- I covered most of the walls with one of my all-time favorite wall coverings, metallic-backed grass cloth. Installation can be tricky because it's really important that the grain be straight, but the shimmery, light-reflecting effect is worth it. Using a laser level helps make sure the first panel is perfectly vertical, and then the remaining pieces fall in line.

- Yiayia makes a mean moussaka, not to mention other Greek delicacies, and she needs her own kitchen to do it. I used the cabinets Marie and Alex had already installed, but I gave them a more modern look with new metal-framed, frosted-glass doors for the upper cabinets. I kept the sink for budget reasons, but replaced the countertop and added a backsplash of glass tiles.

- For the living area, I built out the center section of the wall to put in a focal-point fireplace. The room is too small to use a gas or wood-burning fireplace, but an electric model is perfect. With a 5,000 BTU heater and patented Flammation technology, it will provide both physical and visual warmth!

- Custom-built shelves on each side of the fireplace offer lots of room for display as well as a television. I painted the shelves to match the trim and installed mirror on the backs. The mirror isn't noticeable at first, but it has a huge impact on the sense of space, making the room feel larger.

- In a small space, furniture is all about scale. An apartment-size sleeper sofa is roomy enough to seat three but designed to take up a minimum of space. A pair of my Otis club chairs is great for a small room because they have tight backs and small arms, with plenty of depth for the seat.

- To separate the living area from the kitchen, I brought in a petite pedestal table and a pair of upholstered chairs. This gives Yiayia a place to enjoy a cup of morning coffee or a late-night snack.

- Lighting helps eliminate the subterranean feeling of a basement. In addition to the existing recessed lights, I added accent lighting with under-shelf puck lights, under-cabinet and interior lights in the kitchen cabinets, and a sparkly little pendant fixture over the breakfast table. A few table lamps beside the seating put task lighting where Yiayia needs it.

- To give her some privacy without blocking the only source of natural light, I applied privacy film to the back-door window.

ABOVE: I built out a portion of the wall to install a beautiful new electric fireplace, with a niche above for display. The cocoa-brown color speaks to the tile backsplash in the kitchenette and grounds the room with visual warmth. A curtain screens the room from the hallway and Yiayia's bedroom.

ABOVE: Mirror backing behind the wall of shelves doubles the illumination from under-shelf puck lights, recessed ceiling lights, and table lamps to make the basement living room feel open and inviting. Chairs designed with low arms and tight backs are perfect for a small space.

STYLE ELEMENTS

- To make this very small space feel larger, I used texture, color, and reflections. Subtle texture comes from the grass-cloth wallpaper, which wraps the whole room in cocoon-like warmth. The metallic backing gives a glowy effect that grabs and reflects the light and makes the room feel like a little jewel box.

- The pale-sand color of the wall covering also helps push the walls back, and I kept contrast levels low to enhance that effect. A cocoa-brown acrylic mohair for the sofa picks up a subtle fleck in the wallpaper. Berry-red linen on the lounge chairs and a cocoa and cream carpet add a pop of subdued color for interest.

- Below the wall cabinets in the kitchen, I installed brown glass tiles as a backsplash. The dark color is elegant and modern, and the glassy surface adds depth with its sparkle and shine. I also painted the kitchen wall cocoa brown to balance the color of the fireplace wall.

- For the new kitchen countertop, I chose budget-friendly satin-oxide laminate. It brings in some space-expanding shimmer and shine and looks clean and modern at a fraction of the cost of real stainless steel.

- To screen the living area from the bedroom, I hung a simple grommet-topped curtain on a steel cable.

ABOVE: Yiayia has a separate bedroom, but this apartment-size sleeper sofa will come in handy if other family members visit from out of town. Accent pillows combine a houndstooth check with a berry-color solid, dressed up with fancy beaded trim for a little razzle-dazzle.

BELOW: A little cube of crystal beads brings unexpected sparkle to the mini-breakfast area, where a pedestal table and clean-lined upholstered chairs divide the living room from the kitchenette. Updating the cabinets with new frosted-glass doors is an easy DIY job anyone can do if the cabinets are standard size.

ABOVE: Making the most of a small space is all about scale—and when it comes to artwork, bigger can be better. Filling the corner wall with a large painting creates a sense of depth that draws you in. I anchored it with a pair of woven wicker stools that can double as seating or side tables when Yiayia's family decides they all want to come downstairs to her place!

ARTIST'S AERIE

CHALLENGE

Dawn is an empty-nester who spends a lot of time painting watercolors, but her studio in the basement isn't ideal. Now that daughter Anne is grown and living on her own, Dawn thought her upstairs bedroom would be a perfect studio—it has natural light from two windows and enough floor space for the necessary storage and work surfaces. The hardest part of this makeover is clearing out the room, which has become a messy landing pad for all kinds of stuff! The only pieces that get to stay are Dawn's husband's old desk and a chaise that belonged to her grandmother.

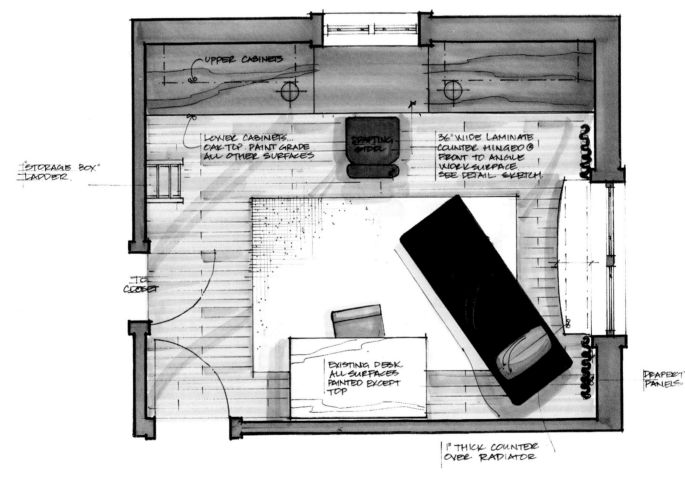

BEFORE: Dawn's daughter, Anne, moved out long ago, but her bedroom is still full of her old books, posters, and possessions. It has also become a catchall for furniture Dawn isn't using elsewhere, including her husband's old desk and an antique chaise.

AFTER: Clean white walls amplify available light, which is crucial for a painter. I placed Dawn's antique chaise (rebuilt, re-stuffed, and reupholstered!) on an angle to free up space for an entire wall of work surface and storage. Draperies frame the window for a touch of feminine elegance.

SOLUTION

- After I got the room cleared out, the first task was to paint the walls. The old wallpaper had been applied over lath and plaster and would have been a real mess to remove, so I simply painted right over it. I primed it first, using an oil-base primer; a water-base primer risks lifting parts of the paper off the wall, creating the mess I wanted to avoid. I applied a soft antique white paint to the walls and the ceiling to reflect the clean, pure light that's critical to an artist.

- I designed a whole wall of work surface and storage. The custom-built desk incorporates open cubbies for storage, slotted shelves for papers, and a vertical cubby for portfolios and boards, all topped by a long countertop with a backsplash. The two wall-mounted cabinets offer more open storage.

- Proper lighting is critical in an artist's studio, and I chose halogen because it puts out a pure white light that gives true color rendition. A halogen track light replaced the old ceiling fixture, and halogens under the wall cabinets wash light down onto the countertop.

- I put the radiator to work too, with a custom-shaped top that matches the work-surface countertop. It's heat-resistant and provides a place for Dawn to rest her palette as she paints by the light of the window.

ABOVE: Slotted storage keeps art papers and finished paintings flat and organized, while a vertical cubby is just the right size for stashing a portfolio. I installed a positionable sconce on the edge of each wall cabinet for soft accent lighting.

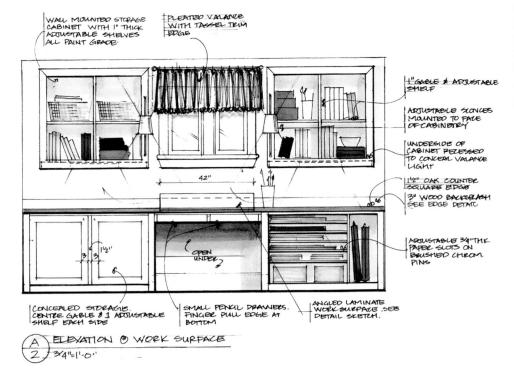

WALL MOUNTED STORAGE CABINET WITH 1" THICK ADJUSTABLE SHELVES ALL PAINT GRADE.

PLEATED VALANCE WITH TASSEL TRIM EDGE

1" GABLE & ADJUSTABLE SHELF

ADJUSTABLE SCONCES MOUNTED TO FACE OF CABINETRY

UNDERSIDE OF CABINET RECESSED TO CONCEAL VALANCE LIGHT

1½" OAK COUNTER SQUARE EDGE

3" WOOD BACKSPLASH SEE EDGE DETAIL

ADJUSTABLE ¾" THK. PAPER SLOTS ON BRUSHED CHROM. PINS

42"

OPEN UNDER

3 ½" 1½"

CONCEALED STORAGE. CENTRE GABLE & 1 ADJUSTABLE SHELF EACH SIDE

SMALL PENCIL DRAWERS. FINGER PULL EDGE AT BOTTOM

ANGLED LAMINATE WORK SURFACE. SEE DETAIL SKETCH.

A 2 — ELEVATION @ WORK SURFACE
¾"=1'-0"

LEFT: You can never have too much storage or too much work surface in an artist's studio. Open cubbies are adaptable—Dawn can organize supplies in baskets or stack boxes of paints and brushes in the openings. A simple valance hung above the window frame makes the small window appear a little bigger. The wall cabinets align with the valance, about 5 inches below the ceiling, for a clean, unified look.

ABOVE: Restored to Edwardian-era splendor, Dawn's antique chaise makes a comfy spot to plan new paintings. Her husband's old desk, revitalized with a coat of paint and new hardware, makes a handy home-office center, and the top is deep enough to use for framing paintings.

STYLE ELEMENTS

- While the walls, ceilings, and cabinetry needed to be soft white so that reflected light would be clean but not harsh or glaring, Dawn's studio needed some color to make it inspiring. I looked to her paintings for guidance, and they said, "Choose a palette of plums, teals, and gold!"

- To restore her antique chaise to its proper glory, I had it rebuilt, re-stuffed, and reupholstered in an elegant eggplant-colored velvet, with a deep fringed trim. Angled in the corner, it's perfect for contemplating a work in progress or maybe for taking a nap (painting is hard work!).

- To bring some feminine softness into the room, I framed the large window with striped silk draperies and topped the smaller window with a matching valance. For light control and privacy at the large window, I installed a plum velvet Roman blind.

- More fabric comes into the room by way of a slipcover for her desk chair, stitched from leftover pieces of the upholstery and drapery fabrics. Who says a desk chair needs to look utilitarian?

- For a unique and handy display system, I mounted three drapery rods on the wall and threaded them with drapery rings that have clips attached. It's perfect for hanging works in progress and newly completed paintings.

- Every artist needs an inspiration board—a place to post photos, postcards, and art that inspires her. I applied fabric in big horizontal stripes to a pin board and hung it on the wall, with a picture light above so it looks like a piece of art itself.

- Dawn wanted to keep the old desk that her husband had used, so I gave it a facelift with a coat of white paint and new, sleek metal handles.

BELOW: I love this system for hanging paintings! Drapery rods with rings and clips are spaced far enough apart to accommodate the largest size paper Dawn usually uses.

UNDER THE EAVES

CHALLENGE

Meredith and Michael are super-busy medical professionals with a young daughter, Lauren. They love the third-story attic of their beautiful 1920s home and spend their precious free time up here, watching TV, reading, doing correspondence, and playing with Lauren. Now that they're thinking about expanding the family, however, this room is going to have to add one more function to the list: guest room. To be ready for the babysitters (oops, I mean grandparents), the attic needs an injection of style and function, stat! Fortunately, I have just the prescription for turning clutter and chaos into a relaxing, stylish, multipurpose space.

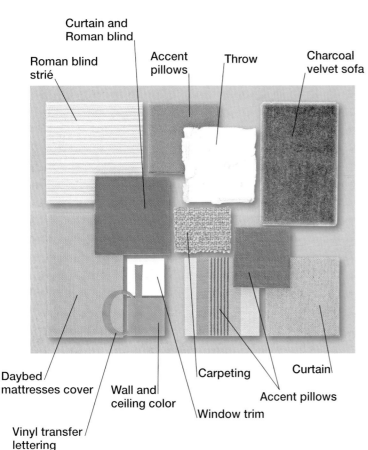

Curtain and Roman blind

Roman blind strié

Accent pillows

Throw

Charcoal velvet sofa

Daybed mattresses cover

Wall and ceiling color

Carpeting

Window trim

Accent pillows

Curtain

Vinyl transfer lettering

BEFORE: Quirky angles can be charming, but this space was falling far short of its potential—in fact, it was a bit of a snooze in the style department. Cluttered with children's toys and a mishmash of outdated furnishings, it wasn't anywhere near as functional and as comfortable as it could have been.

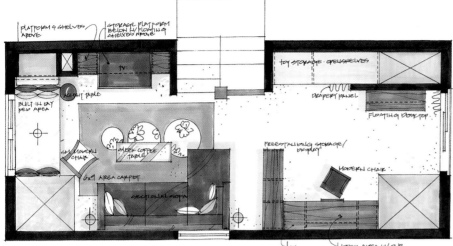

Labels on plan:
PLATFORM & SHELVES ABOVE
STORAGE PLATFORM BELOW W/ FLOATING SHELVES ABOVE
TV
TOY STORAGE · OPEN SHELVES
ACCENT TABLE
DRAPERY PANEL
BUILT-IN DRY BAR AREA
FLOATING DESKTOP
SM MODERN CHAIR
DARK COFFEE TABLE
FREESTANDING STORAGE/ DISPLAY
6x9 AREA CARPET
MODERN CHAIR
SECTIONAL SOFA
FILE CABINET
DESK AREA W/ ONE BANK OF DRAWERS FREESTANDING LEDGE TO SIT ON TOP OF DESK.

AFTER: Breaking the long, skinny attic into zones organizes it by function while keeping sight lines and traffic paths clear. A big sectional with a chaise component defines the relaxation-TV zone at one end, and there's a home office at the other.

SOLUTION

- While all the quirky angles and nooks give the attic character, unifying them with continuous color and low-contrast tones calms the space and makes it feel more expansive. I painted the walls and ceiling the same charcoal gray to wrap the room in a cocoon of color.

- To blend their large television into the room, I designed a new TV-and-storage cabinet that fits into the niche the TV already occupied. Because access to under-the-eaves storage is in the side of this niche, I had to design the unit so that one part is on wheels and can be pulled out if necessary. The part that holds the TV is stationary.

- Across from the TV, I positioned a large, cushy sectional with a chaise at one end. The sofa provides plenty of comfortable seating for Michael, Meredith, Lauren, and visiting grandparents. The chaise also acts as a room divider, defining the TV-and-entertainment zone.

- Between the chaise and the home-office zone, I placed a see-through bookcase that reinforces the division of zones without entirely blocking views. Between the bookcase and the end wall, I added a sleek new desk to serve as a little home office. Michael can work on e-mail at the desk and still be included in the family activities.

- To handle the guest room function, I created a unique window seat/pull-out bed in the TV zone. A nested platform base fits into the dormer and is topped with two stacked mattresses made from 3-inch foam wrapped in polyester batting. By day it's a window seat, and when it's bedtime, the platform pulls out, the mattresses are unstacked, and voilà! A double bed!

- The attic had a little kitchenette that Michael and Meredith never used, so I pulled it out and used that space for a wall of storage for kids' toys.

- The original lighting consisted of long track lights, which just emphasized how long and skinny the space was. I replaced them with individual monopoints to help de-emphasize the narrow proportions. In the guest area, I hung a sparkly little pendant fixture for a surprising accent.

BELOW: A wall-height see-through bookcase provides storage and display space and gives a little privacy to the home office without cutting it off entirely from the rest of the room. Monopoint fixtures illuminate the length of the attic but draw less attention to the bowling-alley proportions of the space than the old track lights did.

ABOVE: An envelope of warm gray wraps the space in a cocoon of cozy color while unifying all the angles and nooks. Between the sectional and the window seat/daybed, there's plenty of comfortable seating for family and visitors. Beautiful Roman blinds stitched from a luscious strié provide privacy and light control when guests come to stay.

STYLE ELEMENTS

- The big architectural feature is the angled ceiling. It takes up a large part of the room, but you can't hang art on it. My solution is to apply rub-on graphics in metallic script, covering the surface with words that relate to the activities going on in this space and their definitions. The text brings in a lot of visual (and conversational!) interest and makes creative use of the angled surface.

- To ensure that the copper-colored graphics would show up well, I chose charcoal gray for the walls and ceiling. I continued the gray tone onto the floor with new cream and gray wall-to-wall carpeting and into the toy-storage nook with gray plastic-laminate shelves.

- Dark-tone cabinetry grounds the monochromatic scheme and gives it weight.

- In a one-color or tone-on-tone scheme, interest comes from texture, and that's where my fabric choices come in: dark-gray velvet for the sofa, chenille for a throw, shimmery strié for blinds, satiny cream for draperies and pillows, and light-toned linen for the daybed mattresses. Plum accents in fabrics and accessories add richness and playfulness and pick up on the warm copper hue in the transfer graphics.

OPPOSITE: Words and definitions relating to family room activities run from one end of the attic to the other, right across the skylight. I love these graphic transfers—you just peel off the top protective sheet, position the transfer on the surface and rub firmly, then carefully pull away the backing. It's much faster than hand-lettering!

LEFT: Incorporating the couple's large television into custom cabinetry makes it feel more like part of the architecture and less visually overwhelming. The cabinetry consists of two vertical shelving units, a low horizontal one for the television, and a shelf across the top that ties all the pieces together. If the couple needs to access the attic storage, the vertical unit nearest the window rolls out.

RIGHT: A modern chair and sleek desk tuck under the ceiling to serve home-office needs. The desk's clean lines are contemporary, but the warmth and beauty of the wood add depth and character to the space.

OPPOSITE: A custom-designed pull-out bed fits into the dormer at one end of the attic. By day, the stacked mattresses and layers of accent pillows serve as a window seat; at night, the platform pulls out, the mattresses are unstacked, and it's a double bed!

OPPOSITE: A simple, grommet-topped drapery panel dresses the sliding-glass door that leads to a Juliet balcony. I even squeezed some function into this narrow space with a reading chair, blanket chest, and display shelves.

LEFT: A nook that had held a kitchenette is now outfitted with laminate shelves to keep all of Lauren's toys organized. A grommet-topped satiny cream drapery panel draws across to hide the toys from view—no more clutter and chaos!

4 INSPIRED BY THEMES

FRENCH COUNTRY WITH A TWIST

CHALLENGE

Tony and her husband have been renovating their house top to bottom, but there's one room left to tackle, and they're pooped. The big walk-out basement has a terra-cotta tile floor and three sets of French doors connecting it to a beautiful garden. Toby would like to use the space as an indoor-outdoor, all-season entertaining enclave. She and her husband love all things French and have decorated the rest of their home in that style. She'd like the basement to feel like a little piece of Provence—but not with the typical blue and yellow fabrics and whitewashed antiques you usually think of with French country style.

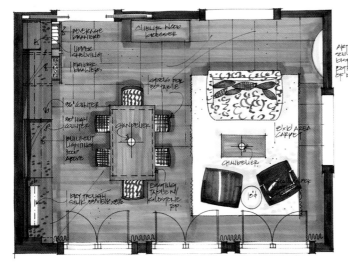

BEFORE: With miles of terra-cotta tile and not much else, the walk-out basement was on its way to becoming a neglected storage area. Toby had big dreams for the space, but after renovating the rest of the house, she and her husband ran out of steam and ideas.

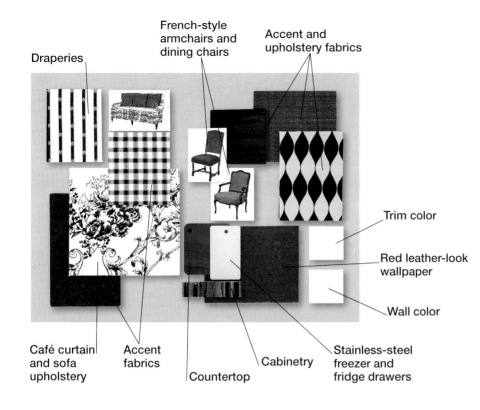

Draperies

French-style armchairs and dining chairs

Accent and upholstery fabrics

Trim color

Red leather-look wallpaper

Wall color

Café curtain and sofa upholstery

Accent fabrics

Countertop

Cabinetry

Stainless-steel freezer and fridge drawers

AFTER: Donning my best beret, I devised an unexpected take on French country style—sort of a bustling French-bistro-meets-Mad-Hatter-party interpretation, with plenty of toile and traditional furnishings in a bold and not-so-typical color scheme of red, black, and white. I call it French country flair with an out-of-the-box, modern, urban edge!

SOLUTION

- This is a big space and will be the setting for parties all year round, so I divided it into two zones: at one end, a casual dining area for light meals, and at the other, an area for conversation.

- The only wall without windows or doors became the feature wall, with a satellite kitchen that will be great for cookouts as well as indoor entertaining. I couldn't put in a sink because bringing water to this wall would have involved tearing up the floor, but under-counter fridge and freezer drawers and a two-drawer beverage fridge will keep snacks, drinks, and party foods fresh and handy.

- A long, two-level counter provides plenty of work surface plus room to set out a buffet. A mix of open and closed storage includes shelves to display Toby's travel treasures. For a touch of French farmhouse style, I broke up the solid base cabinetry with a little curtain that conceals open shelves under the counter.

- To drive home the theme, I accented the kitchen with a modern version of a French country vent hood. Custom-built from wood stained to match the cabinets, it's centered over the curtained storage and aligned with a long display shelf that stretches across the wall.

- The room already had recessed lighting, but it needed a little *je ne sais quoi,* so I installed under-cabinet lighting in the satellite kitchen and two fabulous fixtures in the dining and conversation areas.

LEFT: I love this funky, urban twist on a crystal chandelier! Low-voltage lights beaded along the curvy wires make a little cloud of sparkly light above the dining table.

Chez Toby

Coq au Vin Truffade Soufflé
Tarte Tatin Nougat Glacé Frites

ABOVE: The satellite kitchen along the end wall sets the tone for the rest of the room, with ebony cabinetry and red faux-leather wallpaper. I surrounded Toby's antique table with a typical rush-seat bench and a pair of traditional French side chairs upholstered in not-so-traditional fabrics.

Chez Toby

Coq au Vin Truffade Soufflé
Tarte Tatin Nougat Glace Frites

STYLE ELEMENTS

- The soft green walls didn't really say *"bonjour"* to the terra-cotta tile floor, so I painted all the walls with a creamy hue pulled from the undertone of the tile.

- For the French bistro look, I chose dark-wood cabinets and a black, heat-resistant countertop and backsplash. To set them off, I brought in my secret ingredient: red glazed faux-leather wallpaper. It's a rich, exciting, unexpected finish for the feature wall and provides the jumping-off point for a nontraditional palette of red, black, and white.

- For fabrics, I used traditional French toile, checks, and stripes and revved them up with funky geometrics as accents. Interpreted in black, white, and candy red, the expected fabrics have a fresh, unexpectedly modern feel.

- My approach to a design style like French country is that you can't take it too literally or too seriously. Toby's French table and beautiful antique dresser anchor the dining area, and I paid homage to them with traditional detailing in the kitchen cabinetry and country-style seating. But I tweaked tradition by upholstering the chairs with unexpected, nontraditional colors and patterns, and I chose new pieces that marry traditional lines with modern materials. The coffee table, for example, interprets the characteristic cabriole legs in chrome and has a mirror top.

- Over the dining table, I hung a fabulous lighting fixture, totally not what you would expect—a funky, fun chandelier that's a wild swirl of wires studded with low-voltage lights. Its little brother, a tiny pendant, hangs in the conversation area, centered above the mirror-top coffee table. *Très splendide!*

- To soften the windows and French doors ever so slightly, I hung simple drapery panels in a cute stripe. The rod runs along the entire length of the wall, just below the ceiling, to create a clean, continuous line.

OPPOSITE: To break up the expanse of cabinetry, I dropped the countertop of the center section by a few inches and replaced the cabinet doors with open storage and a toile café-style curtain. Above, a custom-built decorative vent hood recalls traditional French country chimneys. A long ledge stretches out on either side to display some of Toby's favorite treasures.

BELOW: Refrigerator and freezer drawers and a beverage refrigerator pack a lot of practical function into a little under-counter space. Under-cabinet lights play up the rich texture of the wallpaper.

LEFT: Traditional toile covers the love seat, and although the armchair is in the style of an eighteenth-century French fauteuil, its black wood frame and red upholstery give it a modern twist. The coffee table interprets traditional cabriole legs in modern chrome, with a mirror top.

BELOW: A tiny pendant light brings an unexpected bit of sparkle down into the center of the conversational grouping.

SPICY AND SPECTACULAR

CHALLENGE

Eugenia and her family love to celebrate their Mexican heritage with lots of music, lots of dancing, and lots of home-cooked traditional foods. The problem is that the perfect space for their parties is downstairs, in a basement that's a long way from being fiesta-ready. With white walls, non-existing flooring, and random pieces of leftover furniture, it was unfinished and nonfunctional. Eugenia and her daughter, Maricela, wanted the room to capture the vibrant energy and excitement of celebrations back in Mexico—a south-of-the-border–style cantina, but with absolutely no stereotypical decorations like piñatas!

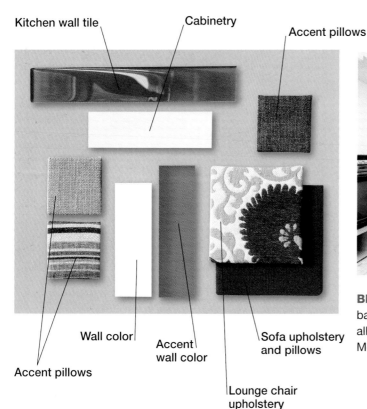

Kitchen wall tile Cabinetry Accent pillows
Wall color Accent wall color Sofa upholstery and pillows
Accent pillows Lounge chair upholstery

BEFORE: This underutilized, under-furnished, and uninspired basement was part TV-room, part storage space, and not at all a reflection of the fun-loving personalities of its owners, a Mexican-Canadian family that loves dancing, food, and fiestas.

AFTER: Now this room is ready to party! A satellite kitchen at one end allows Eugenia to keep food warm and ready for serving. The big sectional seats lots of guests, and when it's time for dancing, the rug rolls up to reveal a durable, dance-ready porcelain tile floor.

SECTIONAL SOFA

COFFEE TABLE

AREA RUG

ENTERTAINMENT UNIT

UNDER-MOUNT SINK

COOK TOP

FRIDGE

SOLUTION

- Since food is such a big part of the family's celebrations, I started with a satellite kitchen that fills the space on one end wall. This zone will be for warming foods that have been cooked upstairs rather than for serious food prep, so a 30-inch electric cooktop and an under-the-counter microwave will do the trick. A small, 13-inch-diameter bar sink supplies water for drinks and minor washing-up duties. I wanted the appliances to be discreet and understated, so I chose a cooktop that's integrated into the countertop for a seamless look.

- Under the counter, I included lots of storage with shallow and deep drawers for dishes, flatware, and party supplies. Behind a paneled door that looks like a storage cabinet, there's a surprise for Eugenia: a narrow, column-style refrigerator!

- All the dancing they're going to do means they need a super-durable floor that's easy to clean and maintain. A porcelain tile that looks just like planks of wood is the perfect solution. To warm the floor and keep toes toasty, I first installed an electric heating pad, then laid the porcelain tile over it.

- For seating, I brought in a big, comfy, L-shaped sectional and a portable side chair that's easy to move when it's time to roll up the rug for dancing.

- When they're not eating or partying, Eugenia and her family enjoy watching TV. Store-bought, ready-to-assemble cabinetry and a big flat-screen TV turn one wall into a media center with storage for CDs, DVDs, and whatever else they might need to keep handy.

- The sectional sits below a tiny window, so to ground the seating and create the illusion of a much larger window, I covered the entire wall with a massive translucent blind. The track is hidden by the bulkhead, and the blinds fall all the way to the floor, adding subtle softness and dimension to balance the hard surfaces in the room.

RIGHT: Hidden discreetly inside the cabinetry, a refrigerator column offers tons of space for beverages and party foods.

BELOW: Clean, modern style meets Mexican-inspired, high-energy color in this cantina kitchen. The microwave sits in a spacious cubby that allows for ventilation, and a trim kit applied to the front makes it look built-in. A small bar sink and an integrated cooktop outfit the kitchen for entertaining. The black quartz countertop and black glass cooktop ground the red tile and relate to the espresso-brown color of the porcelain floor tiles.

ABOVE: A beautiful floral that recalls Mexican textiles inspired the jalapeño-red wall and the gleaming lacquered cabinetry that makes up the media center. Instead of hanging art on the walls, I found a fun vinyl wall graphic that seemed ideal for a room that's all about partying and dancing!

STYLE ELEMENTS

- Mexico is known for its textiles, and a Mexican-style modern floral in chili-pepper red and guacamole green was my jumping-off point for the whole design. A hot, spicy red for kitchen tiles, media center cabinetry, and an accent wall speaks to the exuberant energy of Mexican culture. Espresso brown, black, and white temper the heat of the hue and give the room its modern edge.

- To give the kitchen wall contemporary flair, I chose long, skinny glass tiles in three sizes and installed them in a random, stacked-and-staggered pattern. The horizontal linear pattern also subtly makes the room seem wider.

- To balance the kitchen wall and give some serious kick to the room, I painted the opposite wall in the same sizzling hue. It's the perfect backdrop for some whimsical artwork: a vinyl wall graphic of a dance-step diagram. All of the remaining walls, ceiling, and door got a coat of creamy white.

- Since this room is going to see some serious use with all the parties, not to mention the everyday family together-time, I upholstered the sectional in a super-hard-wearing, family-friendly, 100-percent polyester in a chocolate-mole brown. It's a soft, tactile fabric in a very forgiving color.

- Splashes of pattern add variety and interest to the blocks of solid color. Along with the Mexican-inspired floral on the lounge chair and pillows, I added some visual punch with textured and striped accent pillows in kick-up-your-heels hues.

- The basement has some natural light but not a lot. I installed recessed fixtures in the ceiling for overall illumination, puck lights under floating shelves for accents, and a simple, clear globe pendant in the kitchen that won't block the natural light that streams in during the day.

BELOW: This compact, low-armed chair is easy to move out of the way when it's time for dancing. My favorite room-expander, a tall framed mirror, reflects the sparkle of lamplight and makes the room feel bigger. The translucent, washed-linen blind blends in with the wall, but its soft pleats add some dimension and texture to set off the sectional.

Ready-to-assemble cabinetry in a fiery red lacquer finish serves as a TV and media center. I customized the floor cabinet with new hardware and added puck lights to the floating wall cabinet. A store-bought ebony bookcase adds loads of functional storage in the corner.

BEACH PARTY

CHALLENGE

Paul and Debbie love the fact that their home is just steps away from the beach. Debbie is a former professional beach-volleyball player, and good weather always finds the family out playing in the sand. On the days when the three rambunctious boys can't go outside, the basement is their domain. It's a sprawling, carpeted, toy-filled space that's a dream playroom for kids—but a disaster for adults! Debbie would like to move the kid zone to one side of the basement and reclaim the part you see when you come down the stairs for adults as well as kids.

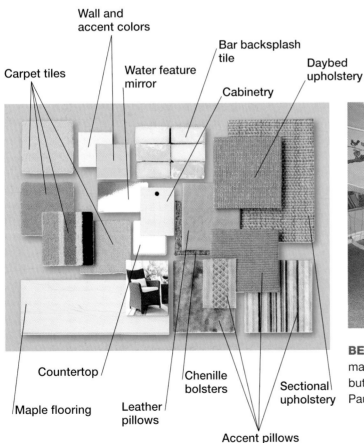

Carpet tiles

Wall and accent colors

Water feature mirror

Bar backsplash tile

Cabinetry

Daybed upholstery

Countertop

Maple flooring

Leather pillows

Chenille bolsters

Accent pillows

Sectional upholstery

BEFORE: Colorful murals and plenty of floor space for toys make this basement a perfect play space for three lively boys, but with all the kid clutter and no adult furniture, Debbie and Paul can't use the space for anything else.

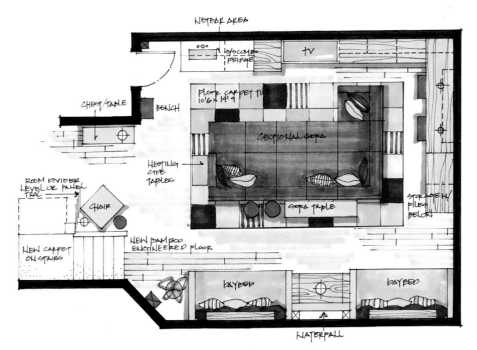

Floor plan labels:
- NEW BAR AREA
- b/scomb FRIDGE
- TV
- CHEST/TABLE
- BENCH
- FLOOR CARPET TILE 10'6 X 14'9
- SECTIONAL SOFA
- NESTING SIDE TABLES
- COFF TABLE
- STORAGE W/ FILES BELOW
- ROOM DIVIDER LEVEL OR PANEL TRAC
- CHAIR
- NEW CARPET ON STAIRS
- NEW BAMBOO ENGINEERED FLOOR
- DAYBED
- DAYBED
- WATERFALL

AFTER: With the kids' toys and playroom moved to the other side of the basement, this half now functions as a beautiful, relaxing room for adults—and as a comfortable family room too!

ABOVE: Maple hardwood floors and cabinetry capture the look of sun-bleached wood, and soft, greenish-blue walls and fabrics bring in the color of the ocean. A snack bar, media center, and tons of storage line one wall, and a pair of banquettes flank a spectacular water feature on the opposite one. A single huge sectional accommodates family and friends comfortably.

SOLUTION

- The first order of business was to move all the boys' toys to the other side of the basement, where they'd be screened from view with sliding woven-grass panels. Then I pulled up all the carpet and laid down maple hardwood floors throughout the basement. The flooring looks fresh and stylish on the "adult" side and is durable and kid-proof for the playroom side.

- Happy as the murals might be for a kids' space, they don't work for the family room. Before I could paint over them, however, I had to apply a primer that cut the shiny finish, and then a tinted primer to cover the mural itself.

- The dropped bulkhead along one side of the room is the perfect place for a long run of custom cabinetry that includes a bar and snack center, a media center, tons of open and closed storage, and a home office area. In fact, I brought in a truckload of cabinetry to solve all the family's storage needs!

- On the remaining long wall, two custom-built banquettes provide seating by day and guest beds at night.

- Between the banquettes, I installed an incredible water feature. The custom-built frame incorporates a huge mirror and a waterfall unit that pumps water up to the top so it cascades down the face of the mirror. It looks like rain on a window, so it creates the illusion of a view outdoors in a windowless basement!

- A big U-shaped sectional fills the center of the room, centered on the big-screen TV, and that pretty much takes care of seating both for family nights and adult gatherings.

LEFT: A countertop that resembles sand or coral frames a funky, wave-shaped bar sink. What could be more perfect for a beach-inspired basement?

ABOVE: Tile that looks like beach glass backs the snack bar area, which includes a bar sink and a beverage fridge. The tall cabinet beside it holds all the music and media equipment. An infrared sensor on the top responds to a remote control, so they can turn on the TV, DVD, radio, or music without opening the cabinet doors.

STYLE ELEMENTS

- Debbie wanted to have the feeling of the beach in the basement, and I was more than happy to oblige! Every element reflects the idea of sun, sky, water, and sand.

- It all starts with maple hardwood flooring—it's the color of sand and establishes a light, bright base for the room.

- Cabinetry is critically important here, because it defines the character of the space. The light color of the wood has a sun-bleached look that brings the tone of the flooring up the walls, enhancing the sunny feeling. Rippled-glass doors resemble water for another beachy reference.

- For the bar area, I found a beautiful countertop that looks like sand or coral and an unusual, wave-shaped stainless-steel sink. The most perfect glass tile goes up as the backsplash—it looks like beach glass! To drive that look home, I sealed the tile with a sand-colored grout.

- To turn each banquette into a comfy daybed, I upholstered a mattress in heavy-duty, kid-friendly woven chenille. Big bolsters covered in the same soft fabric make durable backrests and armrests.

- Accent pillows in caramel leather, deep teal, coral, and a beach-awning stripe help break up the big expanse of solid color on the sectional and add layers of comfort to the banquettes.

- In front of the spectacular waterfall feature, I hung a chandelier made of Capiz shells. The translucent, pearly shells softly diffuse the light of the bulb, and the reflection in the waterfall's mirror is just beach magic!

- To anchor the seating area, I put down a super-practical, super-flexible "rug" of adhesive-backed carpet tiles. They're 16 inches square and come in a multitude of colors. Once you decide on the pattern you want to create, you peel the backing off the adhesive corner tabs and press the carpet square into place. If one gets dirty or worn, you simply pull it up and clean it—or replace it.

RIGHT: A single bulb illuminates a cascade of pearly Capiz-shell discs for glowy accent lighting in front of the waterfall.

ABOVE: As much an architectural feature as furniture, a pair of custom-designed banquettes and a spectacular waterfall installation help define the sand-and-sea character of the basement family room. Remove the bolsters and pillows from the banquettes, and they're ready for overnight guests.

ABOVE: A roomy desk in the corner serves as a home office, with loads of storage on each side. Both the floating wall cabinet and the two-piece floor-to-ceiling unit feature interior lighting and rippled-glass doors that have a watery look. Puck lights in the bulkhead and under the shelves highlight the walls and cabinet faces, and two little pendants bring sparkly light down over the desk.

BELOW: Neat, track-mounted woven-grass panels close off the playroom side of the basement so the daycare décor stays out of sight!

LUSCIOUS LUXURY

CHALLENGE

Jane and Johan are a chic, sophisticated couple who often entertain visitors from Europe—visiting chocolate makers, to be precise, because Johan owns a luxury chocolate factory. Upstairs, their home is charming but small. Downstairs, the basement is big—but not charming! This beige box of a room is full of odd angles and nooks, and the low, awkward ceiling and a column with a partial wall only add to the challenge. Jane and Johan would like to use this space for entertaining fellow chocolatiers as well as storing out-of-season clothing and their wine collection. With lots of chocolate for inspiration, this will be one sweet makeover!

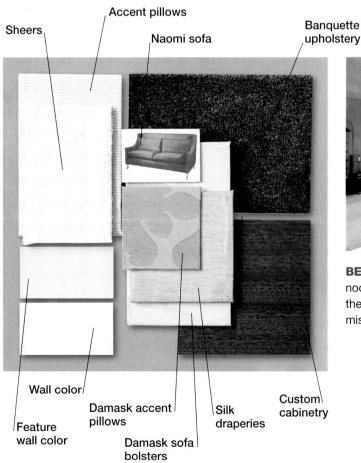

Accent pillows

Sheers

Naomi sofa

Banquette upholstery

Wall color

Feature wall color

Damask accent pillows

Damask sofa bolsters

Silk draperies

Custom cabinetry

BEFORE: This basement was one chopped-up space, with nooks in every direction and an L-shaped column dividing the room in half. Jane and Johan were using it to store miscellaneous furniture and packing boxes.

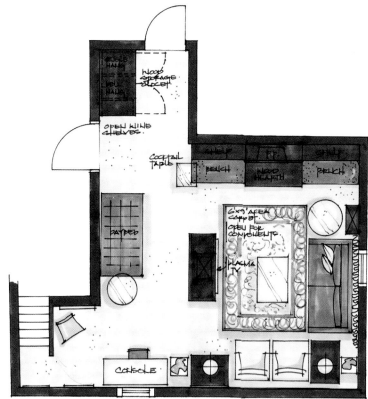

AFTER: Just like the luxury chocolates Johan makes, the basement is now rich and elegant, a stylish gathering place for international chocolate aficionados, as well as family and friends. Tufted banquettes flank a new electric fireplace on the feature wall. I put the column to work as a base for a large-screen TV.

ABOVE: The intrusive support column is now integrated into the room, anchoring the TV-lounging area with a flat-screen TV on one side and music and media storage in one end. A raised electric fireplace flanked by built-in benches creates a gorgeous focal point for the space and gives the whole basement a sophisticated, exclusive-lounge-club vibe.

SOLUTION

- The L-shaped support column was structurally essential, so I used it to my advantage by enclosing it with cabinetry that houses the TV and media equipment. The column also divides the lounge zone from what I call the "wowee" wall zone.

- The basement has a low, awkward ceiling and a tiny basement window, so there are no redeeming features architecturally. That means I needed to create some! Since this room would be a gathering place for European visitors, I created a mood-setting seating area on one wall, with an electric fireplace flanked by big, built-in benches. It's a perfect spot for sipping a little port and sampling some truffles. The fireplace needs no venting and will throw off toasty heat as well as warm the basement visually. Another advantage of electric: I can put in some storage drawers underneath.

- For my second architectural feature, I created a "wowee" wall on the other side of the column. I found some decorative panels with a carved abstract design that reminds me of Johan's corporate logo. I hung them on metal cleats to entirely cover the existing wall.

- In the back corner under the bulkhead, I put in cabinetry that houses the couple's off-season clothing, with racks for their extensive wine collection on one end.

- For seating in front of the TV, I chose my Naomi sofa. Its small proportions suit the space, its high back offers comfy support, and the low arms give more room for sitting. Plus, it has nailhead trim along the arms—love it!

- Simple, tailored chairs with tight seats and tight backs also suit the proportions of the space and round out the main conversation area.

- Lighting brings out the room's new features. Track lights hidden behind the ductwork highlight the sculpted decorative panels, and another set over the fireplace picks up the sheen of the fabric on the banquettes. To create a little focal point beside the sofa, I installed a crystal chandelier over a 30-inch side table.

STYLE ELEMENTS

- The starting point for the color scheme was—what else?—chocolate! Loads of custom cabinetry in gorgeous, dark-stained wood create architectural interest and anchor the scheme.

- The existing beige carpeting was in good condition, so I kept it and used the light tone as inspiration for the wall color. A soft champagne hue smoothes out all the wacky angles in the space and helps raise the low ceiling visually. The dark wood contrasts with this envelope of pale color to create a chic, elegant, modern look.

- To achieve a sort of smoky lounge vibe for the room, I upholstered the tufted-back built-in benches in a heather-gray fabric with a lustrous finish. Black microfiber covers the body of the sofa. Cream damask bolsters on the sofa and creamy lounge chairs pick up the color of the carpet and walls to balance the dark tones.

- For the "wowee" wall, I sprayed the wall panels a silvery gray-blue pulled from the bench fabric. Yes, I said sprayed—that was the only way to get the brushless look I wanted!

- In front of the decorative wall panels, I placed a chaise and plump accent pillows for additional seating when Jane and Johan have really big gatherings.

- The basement had only one tiny window, so I made it disappear behind sheers lined with blackout lining. Dummy panels of silky iridescent champagne fabric frame the sheers, and the whole treatment stretches across 8 feet of wall to frame the sofa.

LEFT: Jane and Johan were so inspired by their new basement, they designed a chocolate bar just for me! Yum!

ABOVE: The wall art on the column says it all! With plenty of seating and surfaces for serving chocolate, the basement is ready for a convention of chocolatiers.

OPPOSITE: The lacy, organic pattern carved into this decorative wall reminded me of the packaging Johan uses for his chocolates. Track lights mounted behind the bulkhead play up the sculpted texture, and a dainty teardrop pendant brings accent lighting down into the room. A chaise plumped with accent pillows in cream and champagne offers guests another place to perch while sampling a bonbon or two.

BELOW: A gallery of artwork greets visitors coming down the stairs. A turn to the left, and they enter the beautiful new space—perhaps picking up a truffle and a cocktail as they pass the buffet! The bench can be moved where it's needed to create more conversation groups.

LEFT: Who would guess there's a dinky little window behind those gorgeous draperies? White sheers and iridescent champagne panels hang from just below the ceiling and make a beautiful soft backdrop for the sofa. I love the way the nailhead trim catches the light! A mirrored coffee table and starburst mirror add more sparkle to the room.

BELOW: Below the electric fireplace, a set of deep drawers doubles as a hearth and serving surface. Drawers under each banquette provide more storage. An elegant, traditional-style crystal chandelier drops low over the side table to create a little secondary focal point beside the sofa.

WRITER'S RETREAT

CHALLENGE

Teresa is a wife, mother, and successful romance writer at work on her third book. After a recent renovation, she finally has a fabulous new room of her own for writing, but at this point it's a big, empty, echoing space that definitely needs some love. In addition to wanting a sophisticated and romantic retreat where her own imagination can run free, Teresa would like to be able to host her writers' group in a comfortable and inspiring setting. I love happy endings—and I know just how to give this space the creative rewrite it needs!

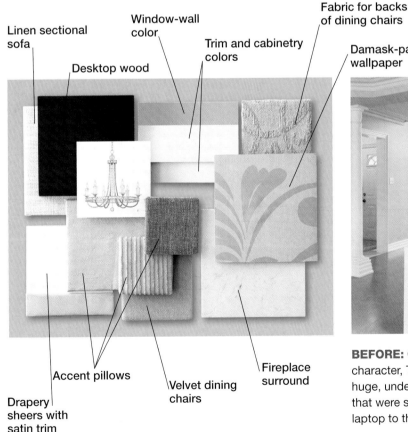

Linen sectional sofa

Desktop wood

Window-wall color

Trim and cabinetry colors

Fabric for backs of dining chairs

Damask-patterned wallpaper

Accent pillows

Drapery sheers with satin trim

Velvet dining chairs

Fireplace surround

BEFORE: Chapter One: Although full of architectural character, Teresa's writer's studio was still a blank slate—a huge, undecorated space with only a lonely desk and chair that were so unconducive to writing that Teresa still took her laptop to the local coffee shop to work.

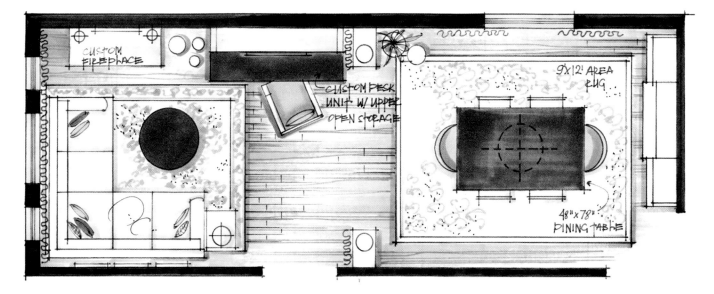

AFTER: Chapter Two: Gorgeous wallpaper wraps Teresa's studio in elegant luxury. Gauzy sheer draperies and a crystal chandelier are all about romance and femininity, and an L-shaped sectional tells a tale of comfort. I know a handsome prince figures in here somewhere!

SOLUTION

- The first thing Teresa needs is a desk—an inspiring desk, with plenty of room to write, as well as storage for all the necessary equipment and supplies. I designed a big, built-in combination bookcase and desk that fills the wall under the dropped ceiling. It's the first thing people see when they enter the room.

- I designated the area under the vaulted ceiling as the writer's lounge, where Teresa and her writing group can share ideas, celebrate successes, and commiserate over rejection letters. To give this area a focal point (and some romantic atmosphere), I installed a beautiful gas-insert fireplace with a stone surround. Nothing says romance like a fireplace!

- An L-shaped sectional tucks into the corner, positioned to face the desk. That way, Teresa can turn her desk chair around and even pull up more chairs if the writers' group expands.

- The other end of the room I designated as a conference room, where Teresa can meet with agents and designers or host workshops. It can also double as a dining room for special family gatherings. I built in a long hutch along the end wall for storage, with counter space for serving snacks, buffets, or drinks.

- To soften the fabulous Palladian windows without hiding them, I hung romantic, gauzy sheers across the entire window wall. The sheers soften and filter the light—and look kind of like a bridal veil! The rod aligns with the base of the half-round window to emphasize the dramatic height of the window.

RIGHT: A component seating system lets me mix and match pieces to create an L-shaped sofa perfectly suited to the space. Accent pillows in luxurious silks, damasks, and velvets play on the spa blue of the wallpaper, with a punch of spicy pumpkin for warm contrast.

ABOVE: A custom-designed desk-and-bookcase combo bridges the two zones in Teresa's writer's retreat—on the left, a gathering space for her writers' group, and on the right, a conference room/dining room (see page 172). All of the shimmery, sparkly finishes and soft, dreamy fabrics were chosen with romance and feminine elegance in mind.

STYLE ELEMENTS

- My jumping-off point for the whole room was an incredible, large-scale floral wallpaper. Printed with metallic silver-toned ink on a pewter-blue background, the wall covering turns the cavernous space into a bold and beautiful, elegant and feminine retreat. The scale of the pattern gives it a contemporary edge, while the design and palette are the last word in romance! For a little visual relief, I painted the Palladian-window wall and the recessed ceiling in the conference room a solid pewter-blue to match the background of the wallpaper.

- The wallpaper also inspired my fabric choices: a creamy linen for the sectional and a silvery-blue solid velvet for the desk chair and two dining chairs. To give the dining chairs a little pizzazz, I upholstered the backs in a coordinating filigree print.

- The new cabinetry and fireplace have the same traditional detailing as the architecture, so they look like they've been there forever. The desk combines function and fantasy—I married a traditional bookcase with a desk that has very feminine, French-inspired cabriole legs—what could be more romantic? A creamy white finish picks up on the room's trim work, and a dark-stained wooden desktop speaks to the dark wood accents that help ground the space.

- The same breezy, sheer fabric that softens the Palladian window also divides the gathering and writing area from the conference room and frames the window in the conference area. All of the draperies are pleated at the top, and because the fabric is so delicate, I beefed up the pleats by stuffing them with polyester batting.

- Teresa's retreat needed mood lighting for inspiration and task lighting for getting words on paper (or laptop). Two antique silver sconces above the fireplace and a stunning crystal chandelier over the coffee table pick up on the metallic sheen in the wallpaper and will inspire Teresa to new heights of creativity. Under-shelf lighting over the desk gives her clear, bright light to work by.

- To bring some sparkle to the conference room, I glued mirrored panels to the back of the hutch and outfitted the cabinets with glass shelves and glass doors. The mirror reflects the Palladian window at the opposite end of the space, making it a feature at the back of the room as well as at the front.

- The room already had beautiful hardwood floors, so I simply anchored the two furniture groupings with large area rugs. The patterns are different but the colors relate, tying the two spaces together.

OPPOSITE: A gas-insert fireplace with a creamy stone surround instantly creates a romantic atmosphere. Two antique silver sconces cast an intimate glow on either side of a French-style mirror. A large, exquisite chandelier that combines crystal, silver leaf, and gold hangs over the coffee table, positioned to reflect in the mirror.

BELOW: A smaller chandelier that's a companion to the one in the writers' lounge hangs over the gleaming, dark-stained dining table. The window in this room isn't a feature, but the draperies fall from just above the window frame to the floor for a formal, elegant look. I painted the ceiling inset to blend with the wallpaper to call attention to the room's architectural detail.

LEFT: Cabriole legs give Teresa's writing desk a distinctively feminine flair. Gauzy draperies mounted on short rods divide the "creative" side from the "business" side of her new retreat.

BELOW: Under-cabinet fixtures shed bright, nonglare light on the desktop and can be controlled independently with toggle switches on the wall.

SPECIAL SPACES

OPEN CONCEPT

CHALLENGE

Rahul and Radhika's new home started life as an icehouse, then became a sign factory before it was converted into a single-family residence. It's their dream home structurally—they love the industrial vibe and the big windows at the back—but miles of terra-cotta tile and a cast-iron wood-burning stove put in by the previous owners don't suit their taste. Their ideal style is modern but warm, with reclaimed and salvaged materials for texture. They've asked me to help them take this loft-like space from an outdated mishmash to a hip, urban sanctuary.

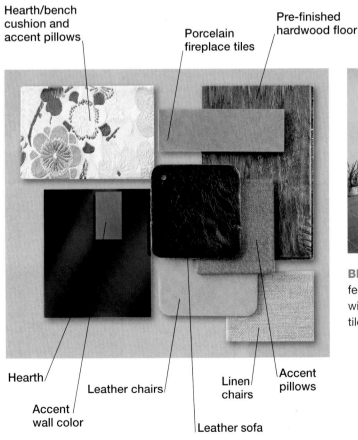

Hearth/bench cushion and accent pillows

Porcelain fireplace tiles

Pre-finished hardwood floor

Hearth

Leather chairs

Accent wall color

Leather sofa

Linen chairs

Accent pillows

BEFORE: Rahul and Radhika appreciated the urban, industrial feel of this old commercial space, and they liked the big wall of windows and the enclosed garden beyond. But the terra-cotta tiles and wood-burning stove just weren't "them."

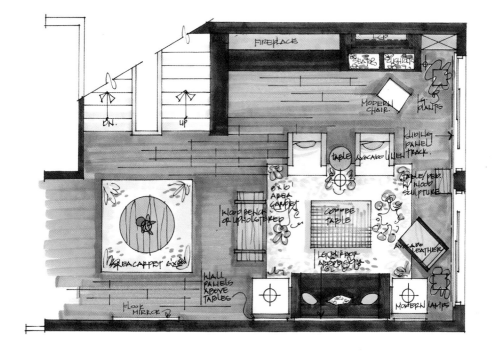

AFTER: Dark-stained pre-finished flooring, comfy, contemporary furniture; and a stunning new fireplace framed in large-format porcelain tile gives the room an entirely different character—chic and modern, yet warm and welcoming.

ABOVE: A rich chocolate wall backs up the chocolate leather sofa and showcases some of the couple's photographs. Soft green on the opposite wall connects to the outdoors and creates an inviting and comforting atmosphere. A large area rug anchors the furniture arrangement, which focuses on conversation and leaves open a traffic path to the sliding glass doors. I outfitted the doors with bi-fold shutters that match the wooden blinds installed in the clerestory windows above.

SOLUTION

- Taking this space from dated and dysfunctional to warm and inviting meant a little demolition and construction were necessary. I tore out the wood-burning stove and chimney and put in a unique statement wall with a fantastic, long, rectangular fireplace. The gas insert eliminates the mess of the old wood stove and will keep the room toasty in winter.

- Getting rid of that dated terra-cotta floor was less messy—I simply covered it up! Because the floor was level and in good condition, I could lay pre-finished wide-plank wood flooring right on top of it. The tongue-and-groove construction is glued and floated over a pad that cushions the flooring from the tile.

- The room had great bones, but simply wasn't working style-wise. The long, narrow space needed to be broken up to feel more welcoming and less like a bowling alley, so I divided it with a long library table. New seating defines the living room at the garden end of the space.

LEFT: The gas fireplace makes a really modern statement, with its long, linear design, stainless-steel frame, and porcelain-tile surround. The TV rests on a floating storage unit that conceals media equipment and echoes the clean, modern design of the hearth and bench below.

STYLE ELEMENTS

- The focal point of the living room is the fireplace, a really modern showpiece. To frame the long, narrow gas insert, I created a sleek, ceiling-high "surround" of large-format, rectangular porcelain tiles in a brown-slate color. A long, low custom bench of walnut-stained wood stretches across the entire wall to serve as a hearth and seating. As the *pièce de résistance,* I installed seven recessed lights in the bench. The square, stainless-steel faceplates make a graphic pattern along the base of the bench and provide unexpected accent lighting at floor level.

- The very modern fireplace sits in contrast to the floor, which looks almost like reclaimed hickory. The antiqued appearance picks up on the reclaimed finishes Rahul and Radhika have chosen elsewhere in their home.

- For seating, pieces from my collection supply the modern style the couple likes, and I upholstered them in a mix of leather and linen for a clean, sophisticated, urban look: chocolate-brown leather for the sofa, delicious avocado-green leather for sling-back lounge chairs, and neutral linen for upholstered armchairs and a bench. Cushions for the hearth/bench seat are covered in a beautiful Asian-inspired floral that brings together the brown, avocado, and cream color scheme and connects to the garden outdoors. Pistachio-green and brown wool pillows break up the expanse of brown on the leather sofa.

- Both Rahul and Radhika are talented amateur photographers, and their vacation destinations are usually dictated by what they want to shoot next. I decided to showcase some of their photos on the room's longest wall, opposite the fireplace. To create a dramatic backdrop for the photos, I painted the wall chocolate brown. The rest of the walls got a fresh coat of soft green, to connect to the outdoors.

- I created a DVD slide show of their photography and set it up to run on a continuous loop on the flat-screen TV. (How cool is that?)

- I replaced the old, ordinary ceiling fan with a terrific stainless-steel model that looks like two antique fans mounted on a supporting arm. The stainless-steel finish picks up on details elsewhere in the room, and the big fan will circulate a lot more air than the old one did.

- To control light and provide some privacy at the windows, I installed wooden blinds on the clerestory windows and added matching wooden bi-fold doors for the sliding doors.

ABOVE: The Otis chair, upholstered in linen, has low arms and a small scale that make it a good fit for tight spaces. A button-tufted brown wool pillow adds color contrast for interest.

ABOVE: Seating from my collection combines classic comfort with contemporary style. The Oscar sofa features luggage stitching, and the Beckett chairs update the mid-century modern sling-back chair. Super-cool, super-contemporary table lamps frame the sofa with columns of glowing light.

SPACE TO CREATE

CHALLENGE

After years of living in an apartment, Ashira and her family have moved into the house of their dreams. It has loads of space, with a bedroom for each child and a study for Ashira's husband. The only one who doesn't have a room of her own is Ashira. She'd love to have a studio set aside for her artwork, and she even has just the spot for it—a huge walk-in closet/dressing room with a big window and lots of storage. It's a space most women would envy, but for Ashira, it's the ideal place to paint.

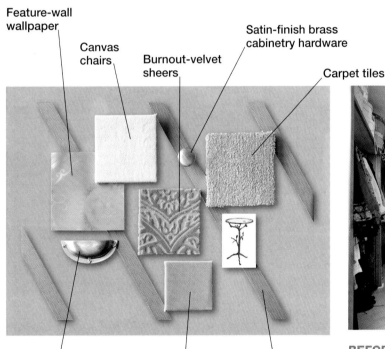

Feature-wall wallpaper

Canvas chairs

Burnout-velvet sheers

Satin-finish brass cabinetry hardware

Carpet tiles

Satin-finish brass cabinetry hardware

Velvet window seat cushion

Pin board ribbons

BEFORE: For many people, this huge dressing room, with its hardwood floors, big windows, and acres of closets, would be a dream come true. For Ashira, it was just underutilized space, and she had a much better purpose in mind.

AFTER: This gorgeous artist's retreat is like a little jewel box off the master bedroom. New creamy white cabinetry and a 12-foot-long brushed-gold counter give Ashira lots of work space and storage. Paint and new cabinetry hardware bring the rest of the room in line.

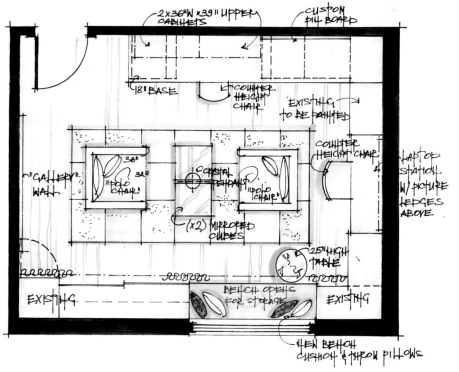

SOLUTION

- Ashira's large master bedroom had plenty of space for free-standing clothes storage, so I brought in sleek new cabinetry to hold all of the clothes that were in the walk-in closet. Then I ripped out the clothes storage in the soon-to-be-art-room and put in one long, continuous work surface with storage above and below for the main painting area.

- The rest of the cabinetry got a facelift with paint and new hardware. The beaded-board doors had to be caulked first to give a smooth surface for painting. Otherwise, the joints between the boards would show up as black.

- The space between the two cabinets on the end wall was perfect for a computer station that Ashira can use as a home office. I joined them with a countertop for a work surface and added a shelf with under-shelf lighting and a desk chair.

- In the center of the room, I arranged a lounging zone, with a pair of beautiful little chairs and two mirrored cube tables. An area rug of carpet tiles anchors the grouping. The carpet squares are a super-practical choice for an artist's studio, because they're easy to pull up and clean or replace in case of spills.

- The window already had a window seat with storage under the lid, so I added a nice thick cushion and some throw pillows.

RIGHT: A brushed-gold laminate counter installed between two existing storage cabinets serves as a home office. Shelves above provide space for a rotating art display.

ABOVE: Under-cabinet fixtures illuminate the work surface of Ashira's creative space, an extraordinary brushed-gold laminate. The big, velvet-covered pin board will keep inspiring images and ideas handy. The original cupboard and drawers, freshened with paint and new hardware, are perfect for keeping papers, paints, and other art supplies organized.

BELOW: An area rug of carpet tiles in squares of blue and cream anchors the lounge area in the center of the room. Petite chairs with nice, tailored arms and legs provide comfy, contemporary-style seating. The mirrored cubes essentially disappear because what you see are reflections of the rug and chairs rather than the cubes themselves.

STYLE ELEMENTS

- Ashira leads a crazy-busy life, and she wants her studio to be a beautiful, calm, inspirational place she can retreat to and create. I established that mood with two feature walls covered in an absolutely gorgeous wallpaper. The exotic, almost hand-drawn quality adds character and modern elegance to the room, and the aqua-blue and metallic-gold colors inspire the whole scheme of blue, cream, and gold for the room.

- I painted the walls, doors, and cabinetry a soft, creamy shade of white to match the new cabinetry that I brought in for the painting area. The 12-foot-long countertop is a laminate in the most beautiful satin-gold finish! New satin-finish brass pulls on all the cabinetry go perfectly with the wallpaper and countertop.

- I upholstered the two lounge chairs with a fabric near and dear to an artist's heart, canvas. The window seat cushion is covered in soft blue velvet, and accent pillows add pattern and luscious color.

- A woven-grass blind provides texture and controls light at the window. For luxurious softness, I framed the window and mirrored doors with nonfunctioning drapery panels in a stunning gold burnout-velvet. The panels form columns of fabric that create an architectural rhythm across the wall. They're delicious!

- For the mirrored doors, I had a burst of inspiration: I had quotations from famous artists printed up as vinyl graphics and applied them all over the mirrors. Now when Ashira looks at them, she'll see nothing but encouragement.

- To give her the best possible light to work by, I installed a series of boxed under-cabinet light fixtures over the desk and fitted them with xenon bulbs. I also extended the room's original 8-foot-long track lighting to 12 feet. And for a totally unexpected element, I hung a spiral chandelier of deep blue crystals over the lounge area. Light is art, art is light!

- Ashira kept an inspiration book of ideas, so I hung a giant velvet-covered pin board over the counter for her to use as an idea board.

- Rows of shelves on one wall allow her to display a revolving gallery of her own work and her children's.

ABOVE: Framed by truly delicious, burnout-velvet drapery panels and softened with a plump, velvet-covered cushion, the window seat offers Ashira a comfortable place to sketch and plan. A spiral of purple and teal crystal beads sparkles over the mirrored cube coffee tables for a fun and creative accent.

" I PAINT OBJECTS
AS I THINK THEM
NOT AS I SEE THEM "

Pablo Picasso

" ABOVE ALL
IT IS A MATTER OF LOVING
NOT UNDERSTANDING IT "

Fernand Leger

PAINTING

" ART WASHES AWAY
FROM THE SOUL
THE DUST OF

LEFT: Three display shelves on the wall showcase a rotating collection of Ashira's and her children's artwork. The gorgeous wallpaper has a lovely hand-drawn quality that's elegant, feminine, and exotic.

OPPOSITE: Quotations by Ashira's favorite artists cover the mirrored sliding doors that conceal a built-in closet. I had the quotations printed on vinyl transfer material. They're easy to use: Just position on the surface, rub firmly to transfer the image, and then peel away the backing.

SECRET RETREAT

CHALLENGE

Brodie is from Australia, where outdoor entertaining is a way of life, so when she and her husband, Tammer, found a spectacular home with a summer coach house hidden at the back of the garden, it was love at first sight. The pavilion was in rough shape, unfinished inside and a little dangerous outside, with an uneven terrace of concrete pavers. But Brodie could see its potential as a spectacular place for barbecues and backyard parties—and so could I!

Bamboo wallpaper on ceiling

Laminate kitchen wall and counter

Embroidered daybed sheers

Cabinetry and wall color

Paisley slipper chairs

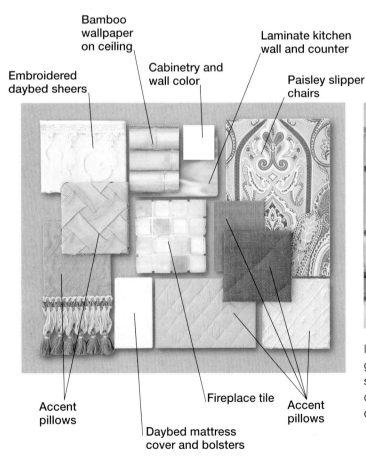

Accent pillows

Fireplace tile

Accent pillows

Daybed mattress cover and bolsters

BEFORE: The coach house hidden away at the back of the garden was unfinished inside and was just being used to store garden furniture and miscellaneous junk. The angled ceiling was rough particleboard that had been painted, and the concrete floor and masonry walls were prone to dampness.

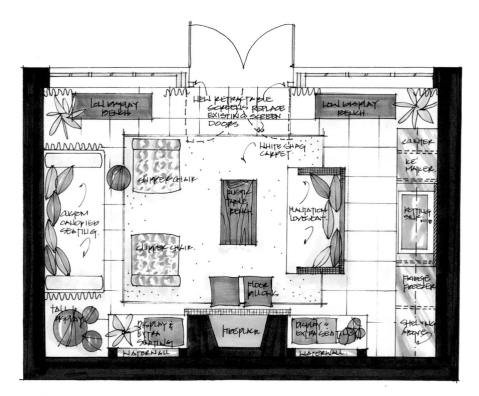

AFTER: A new deck outside and sumptuous, unexpected fabrics and tropical textures inside transform the coach house into an elegant place for entertaining nearly year-round. A luxurious daybed anchors the indoor seating group, which combines comfy upholstered chairs and a casual wicker settee.

SOLUTION

- To make the whole backyard work to its full potential, I cleaned up the surrounding garden, cleared out the overgrowth, and replaced the old concrete pavers with a foundation of bricks topped by a big 16 x 20-foot wood deck. Installed at the same level as the floor of the coach house, the deck functions as a continuation of the indoor space.

- On one side of the deck, I put in a big gas barbecue. On the opposite side, a multipurpose seating area is anchored by a marble table that Brodie found in the coach house and wanted to keep.

- In the center of the deck, I put in a totally cool raised gas fireplace, like a campfire for summer evenings (see page 200). The propane fireplace is basically a shallow metal unit that sits right on the deck. You just drill a hole through the deck for a rubber hose to connect to the propane tank below, pile river rocks around the unit to hide it, and get the marshmallows ready!

- Inside, the coach house had plumbing so I could surprise Brodie with a party-ready food-service center, complete with a compact ice maker, sink, and refrigerator.

- On the wall opposite the windows, I created a truly spectacular "wow!" feature: a gas-insert fireplace flanked by two waterfalls! The waterfalls are prefab stainless-steel units that come pre-assembled. All I have to do is trim around them with molding (see page 199).

- The fireplace anchors the main seating group, and when the weather gets chilly, the party can move indoors and gather around the fire.

- Behind the main seating group, I built a phenomenal tented daybed. Two upright ends, a platform base, and a top piece that hides the lighting create the sense of a room within a room, perfect for cozy conversation — or maybe an afternoon nap!

LEFT: This spectacular laminate features a photographic image of cascading water. I installed a panel as an oversized backsplash to create the effect of water flowing down the wall and onto the matching countertop.

ABOVE: French doors open wide to emphasize the indoor-outdoor flow of the renovated coach house. The kitchen on the far wall includes an under-counter fridge and ice maker as well as a sink. (The cooking gets done on the "barbie" outside, of course!)

STYLE ELEMENTS

- Inside the coach house, I wanted to create an atmosphere that was fresh, tropical, and exotic. I started at the kitchen wall, where I put in an absolutely spectacular countertop and wall panel. Both are laminate with a pattern that looks like flowing water.

- To frame the fireplace, I covered the entire surround and chimney stack with the most incredible iridescent glass tile in tones of watery blue and pale sand.

- I framed the waterfalls with light wood trim for a sun-bleached effect and backed the units with mirror. Accent lights installed in the upper edge illuminate the water as it pours down the mirror—sheer magic! The feature adds a sense of peace and tranquility, and just the sound of trickling water is enough to make you feel cooler on a hot day. These units also act as air purifiers, and in a dry climate, they serve as humidifiers too.

- Instead of the awning stripes or florals you might expect for an outdoor cabana, I assembled an unusual collection of fabrics designed to create an exotic, fresh, Moroccan feeling. A fantastic paisley in tones of coral and watery blue makes the big statement of pattern and color. It covers two chubby slipper chairs and inspires the collection of decadent brocades and embroidered and quilted fabrics for accent pillows. A beautiful, textured linen sheer hangs at the windows to diffuse the hot southern sun. I wrapped the daybed in an elegant sheer with an embroidered detail for a luscious, rich effect.

- To hide the old, rough particleboard ceiling, I put up the most perfect bamboo-print wallpaper. Papering an angled ceiling is not an easy task—gravity keeps wanting to pull the panels down while you're trying to press them into place—but the breezy tropical effect is spot-on and totally worth the effort.

- In place of the old, tiny ceiling fans, I installed new ones with big blades made of palm fronds. Palm fronds against bamboo wallpaper—perfect! I think I hear parrots and monkeys.

- The ceiling beams and walls got a coat of crisp white to make a clean, airy backdrop for all the exotic textures.

- To ward off the chill that is common with a concrete floor, I spread a flokati rug under the seating. Wool's inherent insulating property makes it a natural for situations like this.

RIGHT: Luscious sheer curtains frame the tented daybed, which has its own exotic little pendant to underscore the feeling of a room within a room. A beautiful paisley covers a pair of slipper chairs and inspires all the fabrics for the stacks of pillows.

BELOW: A showpiece feature wall mixes a little fire and a little water. Gorgeous glass tiles in blue and tan reference water and sand, and a pair of ceiling-height water features literally bring in the sound, sight, and cooling effect of water. With the gas fireplace, Brodie can extend her entertaining into the chilly season. A flokati rug anchors the seating group and softens the concrete floor in both summer and winter.

LEFT: Now the coach house feels like a cottage by the sea, with a verandah out front—very Australian! Wicker chairs circle around the campfire, which is actually a propane-fueled unit that sits right on the deck and connects to the fuel source below.

BELOW: The marble table that Brodie found in the coach house comes outdoors to anchor the dining area for this totally renovated and re-imagined oasis.

ONE ROOM, TWO LOOKS

CHALLENGE

At one time, Devra's basement aspired to elegance—you can tell by the architectural detail and the faux-marble paint treatment on the mantel. But now a television sits in the fireplace, and the rest of the space has been totally taken over by her two kids and one rambunctious dog. The basement leads out to a beautiful new swimming pool that's attracting all the neighborhood kids, so it's sort of a pool house as well. Devra would like to reclaim the space to make it a comfortable, cabana-style room the whole family and all their friends can enjoy all year round.

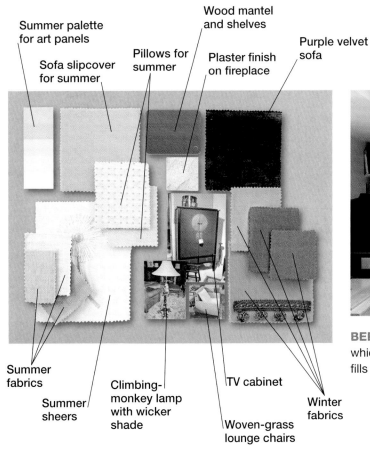

Summer palette for art panels

Sofa slipcover for summer

Pillows for summer

Wood mantel and shelves

Plaster finish on fireplace

Purple velvet sofa

Summer fabrics

Summer sheers

Climbing-monkey lamp with wicker shade

TV cabinet

Woven-grass lounge chairs

Winter fabrics

BEFORE: Kid stuff rules in this walk-out basement playroom, which is otherwise overwhelmingly beige. A nonfunctioning TV fills the fireplace, and another sits on a tall stand.

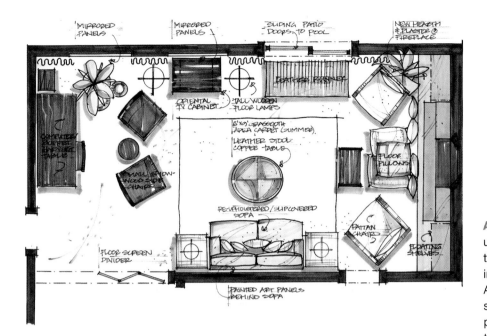

Labels on the floor plan sketch:
- MIRRORED PANELS
- MIRRORED PANELS
- SLIDING PATIO DOORS TO POOL
- NEW HEARTH & PLASTER @ FIREPLACE
- ORIENTAL TV CABINET
- TALL WOODEN FLOOR LAMPS
- LEATHER RUNNER
- COMPLETELY BUFFET BAR/BFT TABLE
- SMALL BROWN WOOD SIDE CHAIRS
- 8'x10' GRASSCLOTH AREA CARPET (GUMMED)
- LEATHER STOOL COFFEE TABLE
- FLOOR PILLOWS
- REUPHOLSTERED/SLIPCOVERED SOFA
- FLOOR SCREEN DIVIDER
- RATTAN CHAIRS
- FLOATING SHELVES
- PAINTED ART PANELS BEHIND SOFA

AFTER: Fresh color, some new grown-up furniture, and a modern makeover for the fireplace turn this chaotic playroom into a serene and stylish indoor retreat. A hardworking leather-topped ottoman serves as seating and a table, and the pie-shaped pieces can be pulled apart to reveal storage drawers.

ABOVE: A new plaster finish and a more modern mantel update the fireplace. To play up the cabana theme, I brought in new seating in woven grass and wicker and layered a woven-grass runner and creamy textured area rug over the existing carpet.

SOLUTION

- After moving all the kids' toys to another area, I tackled this room's biggest problem: the fireplace. I ripped out the old surround and covered the entire wall with a new textured plaster finish. A soft ochre-colored glaze brings out the texture and gives it the look of stone. Getting just the right effect involves liberally brushing on a mixture of four parts glaze to one part paint, then sponging off the glaze with a damp sponge and wiping with a dry cloth.

- New floating shelves fill the recesses on either side of the fireplace. I extended one shelf all the way across to double as a mantel, giving the fireplace a fresh, modern look. A new hearth stretches across the entire wall as well, tying the fireplace and the recesses into a single feature. (And the fireplace worked fine once the TV was removed!)

- To lift the room out of its beige blahs, I bathed the walls in creamy paint.

- I'd love to have had a wall of windows overlooking the pool, but that exterior wall wasn't coming down. To create the illusion of windows, I installed a series of mirrored panels and flanked them with draperies.

- For budget reasons, I kept the carpeting and the original recessed can lights. Simply exchanging the old incandescent bulbs for new screw-in halogen bulbs gives the room a brighter, whiter, more modern light.

STYLE ELEMENTS

- To emphasize the multi-seasonal aspect of this basement family room, I created two distinct looks—one easy, breezy summer look and one richer, more exotic winter look. Everything from the draperies to the pillows becomes part of the seasonal changeover.

- For summer, I chose cheap-and-cheerful, easy-to-clean cotton in light sand and sea colors. For winter, I looked to lush, vibrant, jewel tones of teal, plum, and olive. I kept Devra's old sofa and reupholstered it in lush purple velvet for winter; a pale, gray-blue cotton slipcover dresses it for summer.

- The accent pillows work in reverse—they're stitched from the summer colors and tucked into slipcovers for winter.

- The draperies are pretty ingenious, if I may say so myself! For summer, draperies made from a fun, flower-strewn white fabric hang from the drapery rod that's attached to the bottom of the bulkhead. There's a decorative button on each pleat, and when it's time for the winter makeover, the winter draperies are simply buttoned over the white ones, which serve as a lining.

- To drive home the seasonal color themes, I had three canvas panels painted with horizontal stripes— summer colors on one side, winter colors on the other. They stand behind the sofa and are just flipped when the seasons change.

- In addition to changing the type of light in the old recessed fixtures, I brought in new track lighting over the sofa to play up the art panels. Shallow 20-watt puck lights in the bulkhead accent the draperies and mirror panels. I also put some puck lights over the fireplace and on the underside of the mantel to highlight the plaster finish.

BELOW: Wicker slipper chairs reference traditional garden furniture, but the black finish and seat cushions give them a modern twist. A wooden desk and chair carve out a little home office space at this end of the room.

ABOVE: A soft blue slipcover on the sofa and panels painted in stripes of blue, yellow, sand, and cream emphasize the room's summer look. The nut-brown hue of the ottoman and side tables picks up on the color of the new mantel and hearth and works with both summer and winter palettes.

ABOVE: A beautiful Asian-inspired armoire hides the TV and media equipment. I love the drapery fabric, with its funky little fringed flowers dancing down the panels!

BELOW: Every cabana needs a lamp with climbing monkeys! The woven-wicker shade picks up on the woven-grass chairs and runner to drive home the summer-resort theme.

BELOW: When Jack Frost comes calling, Devra can dress the family room for winter by taking off the sofa slipcover and putting on the pillow slipcovers. Buttoning gorgeous shimmery teal draperies over the summer whites gives the room a jewel-box effect, and a beautiful area rug in a medieval-style pattern pulls the room together in a snug embrace. (Note the fun peekaboo back on the black wicker chair!)

BELOW: Yummy purple velvet upholstery updates Devra's old sofa and cloaks it in winter style. Flipping the canvas panels shows off the cold-weather color scheme.

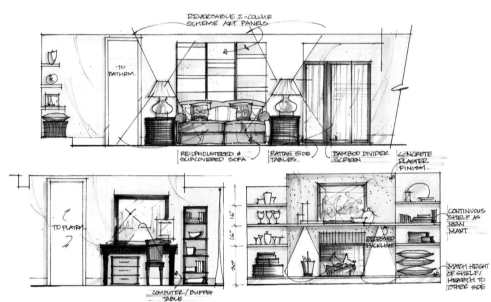

SAFE HAVEN

CHALLENGE

Matthew House offers a safe haven to refugees from around the world. Up to 12 residents at a time live here while making the transition to a new life in a new country, and many former residents and volunteers drop by during the day to help out or to share a meal. Not surprisingly, with so much use, the living room and dining room of this old semi-detached house in the inner city have become pretty worn out. It's my privilege to give this house of new beginnings a fresh start of its own.

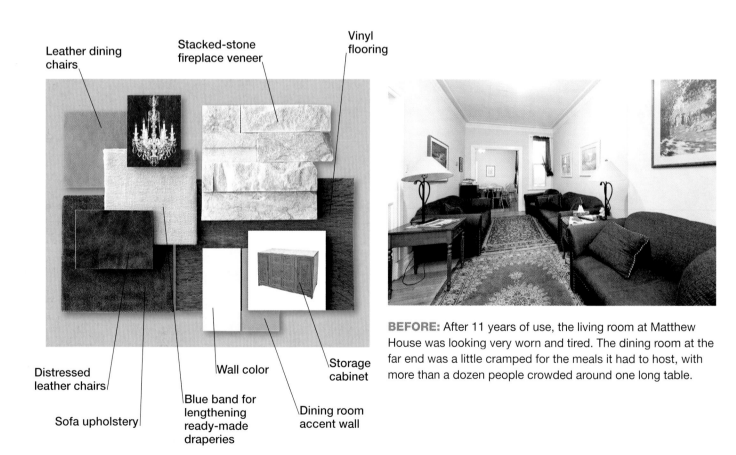

Leather dining chairs

Stacked-stone fireplace veneer

Vinyl flooring

Distressed leather chairs

Sofa upholstery

Blue band for lengthening ready-made draperies

Wall color

Dining room accent wall

Storage cabinet

BEFORE: After 11 years of use, the living room at Matthew House was looking very worn and tired. The dining room at the far end was a little cramped for the meals it had to host, with more than a dozen people crowded around one long table.

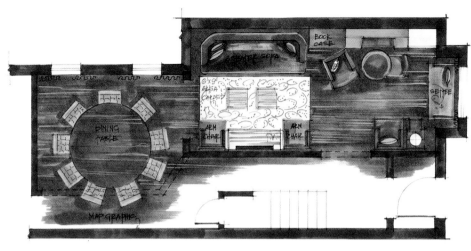

AFTER: A beautiful wall of stacked-stone veneer and an eye-level fireplace now greet residents and visitors as soon as they walk into the entry. The stone says permanence, and the fire is warm and welcoming, a universal symbol of home. The enlarged living room is divided into two seating groups and flows into the dining room through a wide doorway.

ABOVE: Vinyl flooring that mimics old barn board looks timeless and traditional like real wood, but it's more durable and scratch-resistant. The fireplace anchors an eclectic mix of seating that's traditional and comfortable. The little crystal chandelier is literally "a light in the window" to help people find their way to Matthew House.

SOLUTION

- The original dining room was too small and cramped for the number of people who had to eat there, so I knocked down the wall dividing it from the hall to expand it by several feet. I also widened the entry to the living room so you see that space almost as soon as you come in the front door.

- To make sure the first glimpse of the living room was warm and welcoming, I installed a raised gas fireplace surrounded by a wall of stacked stone. Nine feet of stacked stone framing a sleek stainless-steel fireplace that's 34 inches off the floor instantly says "Welcome home." Placing the fireplace at that height means it's visible from nearly anywhere in the room, and it leaves space for a small pedestal table below—an excellent spot for books, magazines, or information residents might need to share.

- Open shelving to the right of the fireplace provides room for storage and display. On the left, I brought in a tall bookcase for more storage.

- The old wood floors were worn past rescue, but I wanted flooring with the warm look of wood. A durable vinyl is the perfect solution—it looks like wood but won't scratch or wear the way wood does.

- The living room needed to accommodate at least 12 people, so I used every nook and cranny for seating: A love seat tucked into the bay window, a couple of upholstered armchairs in the front half of the room, and a long sofa in the back half define the conversation areas, and several little side chairs can be easily moved to where they're needed.

- For the dining room, I found an 80-inch-diameter round pedestal table—the biggest pedestal table I've ever seen! A round table is the best configuration for seating lots of people, but because this one was so big, passing the salt was going to be a challenge. The solution? A custom-made lazy Susan constructed from a square of MDF (medium-density fiberboard) and a turntable base. A large quartz disk is glued to the turntable with silicone.

RIGHT: A second seating group at the back of the living room leads to the communal dining room. While the color scheme in the living room is neutral and serene, the bright accent wall and colorful chairs in the dining room are livelier, like the big meals that are shared there!

STYLE ELEMENTS

- I wanted the first impression to be of safety, security, and stability, so I laid down vinyl flooring that looks like centuries-old, reclaimed barn board. Stacked stone also suggests permanence, and the beautiful warm tones provide the colors for creamy walls and a palette of cognac, charcoal, and brown for fabrics and wood furniture.

- To bring some life to the dining room, I painted the end wall—the one you can see from the living room as well as the entry—a delicious shade of bright blue.

- I laminated the huge city map they'd had pinned to the dining room wall and pasted it onto a wood backing, then framed it with trim screwed directly to the wall (see page 218). Now the counselors and volunteers can write on it with dry-erase markers to show new residents how to get around in the city.

- Beautiful damask draperies were donated for the makeover. The clean, neutral hue blends beautifully with the walls and will have longevity in terms of style. The only problem was, they were made for 8-foot ceilings, and the ceiling at Matthew House is 9 feet. So I added a deep band in soft blue linen for a high-end custom look.

- I chose an eclectic mix of seating to keep the rooms from looking like a furniture gallery. Cute little Louis chairs, a huge spoon-back four-seater sofa, a traditional tufted-back love seat, and some distressed-leather upholstered chairs create a layered look unified by color. In the dining room, chairs upholstered in parsley-green leather add a punch of lively hue.

- Lighting is hugely important here, giving elegance and dignity to both the living room and the dining room. A mini-chandelier in the bay window can be enjoyed from inside and also speaks to people outside, like a beacon that signals a safe harbor. In the back half of the living room, I installed a pair of crystal sconces to frame a new wall-mounted flat-screen TV. In the dining room, a huge crystal chandelier hangs above the table. With something like 300 crystals that had to be attached individually, it makes a stunning impression!

- I hung a big framed mirror on the accent wall in the dining room, to reflect the beautiful chandelier and expand the sense of space.

ABOVE: Creamy walls set off the brown velvet of the spoon-back sofa and the dark wood of the bookcase, creating a high-contrast scheme that feels both grounded and serene. The long sofa can seat at least four people for TV watching or conversation. Accent pillows break up the expanse of solid color with lively hues and patterns.

OPPOSITE: The television is mounted on a swivel bracket so it can turn to face the front part of the living room. The antiqued blue console below provides lots of storage for DVDs and games. A pair of Louis armchairs reference a historic style but have a contemporary look with their black paint finish and charcoal upholstery.

OPPOSITE: Moving the side wall over a few feet made room for an 80-inch-diameter pedestal table. Upholstered leather chairs are comfortable and easy to clean. New track lights illuminate the laminated and framed city map that's both a practical teaching aid and wall art.

BELOW: With the wall removed, the dining room is now open to both the living room and the hall to the front door. The gorgeous, elegant chandelier extends a magnificent welcome to everyone entering Matthew House.

INDEX